THE CREATIVE LUNCH BOX

Coleen and Bob Simmons

To Chet
with Love,
Coleen &
Bob Simmons
6/90

A Nitty Gritty® Cookbook

© 1989, Bristol Publishing Enterprises, Inc., P.O. Box 1737, San Leandro, California 94577. World rights reserved. No part of this publication may be reproduced by any mechanical, photographic, or electronic process, or in the form of a phonographic recording, nor may it be stored in a retrieval system, transmitted, or otherwise copied for public or private use without prior written permission from the publisher.

Printed in the United States of America.

ISBN 0-911954-94-5

Production Consultant:
    Vicki L. Crampton
Photographer: Kathryn Opp
Food Stylist:
    Carol Cooper Ladd
Assistant to Food Stylist:
    Barbara Brooks
Illustrator: Carol Webb Atherly

Table of Contents

METRIC CONVERSION CHART

Liquid or Dry Measuring Cup (based on an 8 ounce cup)
1/4 cup = 60 ml
1/3 cup = 80 ml
1/2 cup = 125 ml
3/4 cup = 190 ml
1 cup = 250 ml
2 cups = 500 ml

Liquid or Dry Measuring Cup (based on a 10 ounce cup)
1/4 cup = 80 ml
1/3 cup = 100 ml
1/2 cup = 150 ml
3/4 cup = 230 ml
1 cup = 300 ml
2 cups = 600 ml

Liquid or Dry Teaspoon and Tablespoon
1/4 tsp. = 1.5 ml
1/2 tsp. = 3 ml
1 tsp. = 5 ml
3 tsp. = 1 tbs. = 15 ml

Temperatures

°F		°C
200	=	100
250	=	120
275	=	140
300	=	150
325	=	160
350	=	180
375	=	190
400	=	200
425	=	220
450	=	230
475	=	240
500	=	260
550	=	280

Pan Sizes (1 inch = 25mm)
8-inch pan (round or square) = 200 mm x 200 mm
9-inch pan (round or square) = 225 mm x 225 mm
9 x 5 x 3-inch loaf pan = 225 mm x 125 mm x 75 mm
1/4 inch thickness = 5 mm
1/8 inch thickness = 2.5 mm

Pressure Cooker
100 Kpa = 15 pounds per square inch
70 Kpa = 10 pounds per square inch
35 Kpa = 5 pounds per square inch

Mass
1 ounce = 30 g
4 ounces = 1/4 pound = 125 g
8 ounces = 1/2 pounds = 250 g
16 ounces = 1 pound = 500 g
2 pounds = 1 kg

Key   (America uses an 8 ounce cup — Britain uses a 10 ounce cup)

ml = milliliter
l = liter
g = gram
K = Kilo (one thousand)
mm = millimeter
m = mill (a thousandth)
°F = degrees Fahrenheit

°C = degrees Celsius
tsp. = teaspoon
tbs. = tablespoon
Kpa = (pounds pressure per square inch)
   This configuration is used for pressure
   cookers only.

Metric equivalents are rounded to conform to existing metric measuring utensils.

Introduction

There are many reasons to carry a lunch box. Whether the need is economic, special diet, time, or nonavailability of prepared food nearby, many people find it desirable to take a lunch with them. Children and older students frequently carry their lunches to school.

Modern "fast food" outlets serve food that tastes good at reasonable prices, but soon become boring in their sameness. They often achieve their good taste by the use of excessive fat and salt, not by using the freshest ingredients and bold flavorings.

With a well stocked pantry, a little planning and a minimum of effort you can pack a lunch box that is much more satisfying than anything that might be available to you near your place of work.

Equipment

Brown paper bags or the classic bread-loaf-shaped lunch box aren't the only game in town. Most hardware, drug or variety stores have shelves of equipment to help get your lunch to its destination in perfect condition. There are many different sizes and colors of vacuum bottles with narrow or wide mouths, dishwasher-safe plastic containers with lids, soft-sided, insulated small and large totes, and attractive molded plastic lunch boxes with specially designed food containers. Some of the lunch boxes have a special bottle to hold your noncarbonated beverage that can be placed in the freezer overnight.

Buy a pretty lunch box or small insulated bag and pack it with real cutlery, a couple of cloth napkins and a glass or cup for your beverage. Use one of the napkins for an impromptu placemat. Another practical investment would be a couple of small "blue ice" pillows to keep in your freezer to add to your lunch to keep it nice and cool.

Be sure to practice good sanitation and wash your food containers and utensils after every use. Wipe out your tote bag or lunch box regularly too. Vacuum bottles will generally keep cold foods in the "safe" zone (under 40°) if both food and bottle are chilled for several hours in the refrigerator. The bottle can be pre-chilled by adding ice cubes for a few minutes before adding the food. Hot foods will stay above 140° for several hours if the bottle is pre-heated with boiling water for a few minutes before adding the food. Store clean vacuum bottles with lids unscrewed. Sharp objects can puncture plastic or break the glass in a vacuum bottle and destroy its insulating qualities.

Pamper yourself. Find a sunny bench or a spot with a view to enjoy your lunch. A change of scene, some fresh air and a delicious lunch can make so much difference in how you feel mentally and physically.

The Pantry

With a little planning you can always have the basic ingredients for a delicious and nutritious lunch in your pantry or cupboard. These canned or packaged items can supplement the best seasonal fresh fruits and vegetables from the market. Here is a basic list of foodstuffs to help you select items to stock your pantry.

Vinegars

Vinegar keeps indefinitely and different vinegars have such distinctive characters that they can contribute significantly to the overall appeal of a dish. As a minimum you could keep apple cider vinegar, red wine vinegar, rice wine vinegar (unsweetened), sherry wine vinegar and balsamic vinegar. The rice wine and balsamic vinegars are generally less sharp. Apple cider vinegar is a good all-purpose substitute in most of our recipes.

Oils

Recent studies tend to show that olive oil is more healthful than other oils. It also has more flavor. You should keep two olive oils in the pantry: a light all-purpose oil for cooking and baking and a fruity full-flavored oil for salad dressings or last minute addition to a dish. The latter are usually labeled "extra virgin" and have a wonderful green or gold color. Extra virgin olive oil tends to change character when open bottles are kept for a long time, so buy small bottles if you find you are using the same bottle for several months. Olive oil should be stored tightly capped in a cool dark spot in your pantry.

The other oil for your cooking should be a vegetable or peanut oil with very low saturated fat.

Chicken Stock

The very best chicken stock is the one you make yourself because you can control the salt and quality. Every basic cookbook has complete instructions and you can make it as rich and thick as you like. Freeze your homemade stock in 1-cup portions and you will always be able to make a soup or sauce on a moment's notice. If you are out of homemade stock use one of the reduced sodium, canned, clear chicken broths. Even with ⅓ less sodium than the regular canned broth, they still have a much higher sodium content than homemade.

Mustards

Unless you eat a lot of hot dogs there is no reason to use the yellow "ballpark" or brown mustard exclusively. Try to always have Dijon and a stone ground grainy mustard on hand. Creole mustard adds a special character to sandwiches and sauces, or try one of the numerous flavored mustards available. A well chosen mustard adds a great deal to the character of a dish but not much to the cost.

Mayonnaise and Dairy Products

The reduced calorie mayonnaise currently available is so similar in taste to the regular product that there is no reason not to use it, particularly if you are adding mustard, herbs, pickles or other flavors to the dish. Try several of the brands available to find one that tastes best to you.

We find the lower fat light cream cheese and sour cream available in the dairy case to be very acceptable in taste and spreadability. They were used in testing these recipes, as were "2%-ten" milk and lowfat yogurt. Ricotta cheese, string cheese, and light or part-skim mozzarella are other healthful products to keep in the refrigerator.

Canned and Packaged Goods

Water-packed tuna fish, canned clams, reduced salt garbanzo and kidney beans, cannellini beans, roasted red peppers or pimientos and ready-cut peeled tomatoes are basic pantry items to be used in many different ways.

Keep rice, several different shapes of dried pasta and a can or two of small cooked potatoes on hand as a base for quick hearty salads.

Frozen bread dough in 1 lb. packages, puff pastry, fresh wonton wrappers and Chinese style noodles keep well in the freezer and refrigerator. Armenian cracker bread is great for Aram sandwiches and can be broken into pieces and used for crackers. A variety of crackers such as Ryecrisp, Wasabread, Cracklebred and wholemeal biscuits are great to have on hand. Pita breads are so very versatile; stuff them fresh or keep them in the freezer, or bake until they are crisp and store in an airtight container.

Sweet and dill pickles, green and black olives, pickled beets, sweet or piquant canned whole peppers, and a small jar of black olive paste make great lunch accents.

Nutrient Analysis

This book offers the added advantage of giving nutritional information for each recipe. Data has been rounded to the nearest whole number. While the latest data from the USDA* has been used, you should use good judgment in applying the nutritional information, especially when special dietary needs or serious health problems are involved. Fat and cholesterol content can vary widely depending on the quality of starting ingredients and the care taken in pouring off excess fat. Sodium content can vary from brand to brand of canned goods, especially for chicken broth. Persons on restricted sodium diets should make their own chicken stock. This is the sure way to know the exact quantity of sodium added to a dish.

In keeping with current trends, we do not specify the quantity of salt to be added to most recipes. When the amount of salt is not specified the quantity of sodium in the nutritional analysis will be followed by a ``+''. Persons on a restricted sodium diet will then be free to add as much or little salt as they desire.

*Recipes analyzed using *The Food Processor II* program from ESHA Research.

Cook on the Weekend for Easy Weekday Lunches

Many of these recipes can serve a dual purpose, providing snacks or dinners on the weekend with "planned-overs" for next week's lunch box. Consider doubling the recipes and putting individual portions in a plastic container or wrapper, and refrigerating or freezing for an easy lunch on those rushed mornings. The chicken dishes can be frozen in individual portions and will help keep the lunch box cool, but ready to eat in 4 hours.

Here are some good choices for the weekend cook:

Leek and Potato Soup, page 16
Gazpacho, page 24
Dolmas, page 80
Hummus bi Tahini, page 88
Marinated Mushrooms, page 92
Teriyaki Beef Rollups, page 98
Caponata, page 76

West Indian Marinated Fish, page 74
Jumbo Tuna and Cheddar Shells, page 83
Handpies, page 116
Honey Glazed Chicken Legs, page 60
Orange Glazed Chicken Wings, page 58
Grilled Flank Steak, page 108

The Creative Lunch Box for Kids

The younger set will enjoy the hundreds of lunch ideas in this book. In addition, we offer special lunch ideas just for them. Pack food that is easy to handle and remember to scale down the size of the sandwiches.

- Send hot macaroni in a vacuum bottle.
- Send a vacuum bottle filled with hot chocolate and a separate package of marshmallows on blustery days.
- Hot soup with oyster or animal crackers is a good vacuum bottle choice.
- Spread a mini pita pocket with peanut butter and fill with grated carrots and raisins.
- Cut one end off a small soft roll, hollow it out and fill it with tuna, chicken or egg salad.
- Handpies are easy to eat and different fare.
- Use cookie cutters to cut bread into fancy sandwich shapes.
- Use a nut bread with a cheese spread instead of white or wheat.
- Thin sliced sandwich bread can be spread with a filling and rolled as easily as making a traditional sandwich.
- Sandwiches cut into 4 pieces are more manageable than 2 larger pieces.

- Make lunch kebobs with square pieces of cheese, ham cubes, olives or pickle chunks, cherry tomatoes or radishes on wooden skewers.
- Include one of the individually wrapped string cheeses or another favorite kind.
- Use flat wide pieces of celery and fill them with peanut butter, placing a row of raisins or whole peanuts down the center.
- Send raw vegetable sticks with a little cup of dip.
- Dice raw vegetables or fruit and combine with cottage cheese.
- Pack a small baked apple filled with raisins and nuts.
- Tuck a little package of dried fruit or raisins in the lunch box.
- Include an individual canned fruit or pudding cup.
- Cut up juicy fruit and send it in a little cup with a spoon.
- Chocolate or lemon icing between graham crackers is an old fashioned treat.
- Add an individual package of fruit juice, complete with a straw. Freeze first and it will keep the rest of the lunch nice and cool.

Be Creative with Light Lunches

If you are watching calories, there are many delicious things to take for lunch. We offer some ideas:

- Alternatives to bread include rice cakes, light mini pitas, lettuce wrappers, tomato or pepper shells, bread sticks or **Crisp Pita Chips**, page 90.
- Reduced calorie mayonnaise or light cream cheese are lower in calories and fat.
- Make a sandwich spread with light cream cheese mixed with bits of chopped fresh vegetables.
- Take marinated cooked vegetables and a slice or two of **Perfect Poached Chicken**, page 56.
- **Caponata**, page 76, is made with very little oil, fresh vegetables and water packed tuna, a good low calorie choice.
- Pack two or three kinds of fresh fruit to eat with some string or other low fat cheese.
- Cold soups such as **Gazpacho**, page 24, or **Cold Lemon Soup**, page 15, taste great on hot days.
- Take a small container of **Chicken and Red Pepper Paté**, page 61, to spread on slices of cucumber.

- Pack a small piece of **Perfect Poached Salmon**, page 65, with **Dad's Favorite Marinated Cucumbers**, page 44, and some thin dark rye bread.
- **Teriyaki Beef Rollups**, page 98 , with **Marinated Mushrooms**, page 92, or **Orange and Fennel Salad**, page 54, go well together.
- Try crisp vegetable sticks or blanched asparagus with a small container of dip.
- **Shrimp Salad**, page 86, is great in a lettuce leaf, stuffing for a tomato or jumbo shells.
- Take a half of a papaya and fill with fresh fruits and a squeeze of lime juice. Accompany with thinly sliced nutbread spread with light cream cheese.
- A large artichoke filled with shrimp and light sour cream or the smallest amount of reduced calorie mayonnaise is a filling lunch.
- Fill a lettuce leaf or two with thinly sliced roast pork and lowfat yogurt mixed with mustard.
- Make a delicious salad of cubed cooked chicken, papaya, celery and walnut pieces. Dress with a little orange lowfat yogurt.
- Toss a cup of warm cooked pasta radiatore or corkscrew shapes with lemon juice, full-flavored olive oil, fresh tomato pieces, sweet basil leaves and lots of freshly ground black pepper.
- Take one half of a **Stuffed Potato**, page 140.
- Combine fresh grapefruit and orange segments with strawberry slices. Drizzle with orange juice and a little honey.

Soups

Consider taking soup for your lunch. It is versatile and can be a terrific addition to your lunch box or a complete meal in itself. Take it in a vacuum bottle piping hot, or add a couple of ice cubes to the vacuum bottle to keep it nice and cool for those hot days. With a microwavable container, hot soup for lunch is simpler yet. Crisp tortilla chips, cracker bread or breadsticks, and some fruit or cookies will round out a very satisfying lunch box.

We have included a **Leek and Potato Soup** that is the base for several different soups. Make it on the weekend, freeze some, and have it on hand for a quick variation. Several of the soups in this chapter are good either hot or cold; take your choice depending on whim and weather. **Gingered Orange Carrot Soup** and **Spicy Tomato Soup** are tasty at either temperature. The addition of pieces of cooked chicken, sausages, croutons or oyster crackers can make a heartier version for those who like a substantial soup.

Cookie Cutter Sandwiches (page 8) ▶

Cold Lemon Soup

Put in a vacuum bottle with 2 or 3 ice cubes for a delicious cooling lunch on a hot day.

6 cups chicken stock
⅓ cup uncooked rice
3 eggs

⅓ cup lemon juice
finely ground white pepper
1 lemon, thinly sliced

Combine chicken stock and rice in a large saucepan. Bring to a boil. Cover and simmer until rice is tender, about 15 minutes. Remove from heat. Beat eggs in a separate bowl until pale yellow. Slowly beat in lemon juice; add white pepper. Carefully stir some of the hot broth into the egg-lemon mixture, beating continuously. Add egg-lemon mixture to remaining broth. Cool and refrigerate. Serve very cold with one or two lemon slices as garnish for each serving. Thickness of soup will depend on richness of chicken stock. Stir well before ladling into cups or dishes.

Nutritional information per serving 115 calories, 4 grams fat, 1 gram saturated fat, 1 gram polyunsaturated fat, 2 grams monounsaturated fat, 9 grams protein, 11 grams carbohydrate, 105 mg cholesterol, 810+ mg sodium

Leek and Potato Soup

It takes less than an hour to make this soup, which is delicious on its own and can be used as a base for many tantalizing variations. The sodium content shown is based on the use of canned chicken broth. You will get a better tasting soup with much less sodium if you use homemade chicken stock. The thickness of the soup depends on the richness of the stock.

3 tbs. butter
4 cups leeks, coarsely chopped (about 3 large)
4 cups potatoes, thinly sliced (about 3 large)
2 medium stalks celery **or** 1 fennel bulb, thinly sliced
6 cups chicken stock
finely ground white pepper
chopped parsley **or** chopped chives **or** chopped canned green chilies and
    fresh cilantro for garnish

Cut leeks in half, separate leaves and wash well to remove sand. Coarsely chop white part. Use a thin slicing blade in the food processor to slice potatoes. Melt butter in a large heavy pot. Sauté leeks and celery or fennel for about 5 minutes to soften. Add sliced potatoes and chicken stock. Bring to a boil, cover and simmer over low heat for about 20 minutes until potatoes are tender. Let cool a few minutes and puree a small batch at a time in the food processor or blender. Add salt and pepper to taste. Garnish with chopped parsley or chives.

Nutritional information per serving 115 calories, 4 grams fat, 2 grams saturated fat, .5 grams polyunsaturated fat, 1 gram monounsaturated fat, 4 grams protein, 15 grams carbohydrate, 10 mg cholesterol, 510 mg sodium

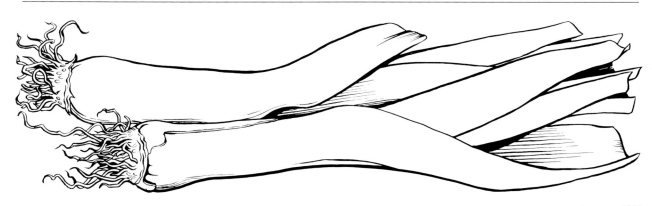

Vichyssoise

*This creamy and elegant cold soup uses **Leek and Potato Soup** for a base.*

2 cups **Leek and Potato Soup**, page 16
½ cup heavy cream
chopped chives for garnish

Stir cream into **Leek and Potato Soup**. Chill several hours in refrigerator. Garnish with chopped chives and serve very cold.

Nutritional information per serving 250 calories, 21 grams fat, 13 grams saturated fat, 1 gram polyunsaturated fat, 6 grams monounsaturated fat, 4 grams protein, 13 grams carbohydrate, 73 mg cholesterol, 410 mg sodium

---

Clam Chowder

*This variation of **Leek and Potato Soup** makes a quick nutritional lunch. Be sure to strain the clam juice through a paper towel in a sieve to catch the sand.*

2 cups **Leek and Potato Soup**, page 16
1 (6½ ozs.) can chopped clams with juice
dash Tabasco
chopped parsley for garnish

Heat basic soup, clams, clam juice and Tabasco. Garnish with parsley and serve hot.

Nutritional information per serving 175 calories, 5 grams fat, 2 grams saturated fat, 1 gram polyunsaturated fat, 1 gram monounsaturated fat, 18 grams protein, 14 grams carbohydrate, 45 mg cholesterol, 450+ mg sodium

---

Quick Corn Chowder

Some corn and ham or bacon make this a cold day treat. Chopped red or green fresh pepper pieces are good for color and taste.

2 cups **Leek and Potato Soup**, page 16
1 (7 ozs.) can whole kernel corn, drained
½ cup cooked ham, diced, **or** 2 strips cooked bacon, crumbled
chopped red or green peppers for garnish

Heat basic soup together with corn. Garnish with ham pieces or bacon and serve hot. Sprinkle a tablespoon of chopped red or green peppers on the soup for a pretty presentation.

Nutritional information per serving 145 calories, 4 grams fat, 2 grams saturated fat, 1 gram polyunsaturated fat, 1 gram monounsaturated fat, 5 grams protein, 24 grams carbohydrate, 8 mg cholesterol, 550+ mg sodium

Curried Pea Soup

This soup is a glorious green color with a light taste of curry, and it is delicious served either hot or cold.

2 cups **Leek and Potato Soup**, page 16
1 (10 ozs.) pkg. frozen green peas
1 tbs. butter
2-3 green onions, thinly sliced
½ tsp. curry powder

¾ cup milk
salt and freshly ground pepper
chopped chives and shredded
  carrot for garnish

Combine frozen green peas, butter, green onions and curry powder in a microwave dish. Cover and cook in a microwave oven about 5 minutes on high until peas are cooked. Combine basic soup, peas and milk in a food processor or blender and process until smooth. Season with salt and pepper. Heat and serve hot, or chill several hours in refrigerator if serving cold. Garnish with chopped chives and a little shredded carrot.

Nutritional information per serving 160 calories, 6 grams fat, 4 grams saturated fat, .5 grams polyunsaturated fat, 2 grams monounsaturated fat, 7 grams protein, 20 grams carbohydrate, 17 mg cholesterol, 355 mg sodium

Gingered Carrot and Orange Soup

The carrot and orange flavors blend beautifully with a little zip of fresh ginger and hot pepper flakes. Serve hot or cold. The food processor makes quick work of slicing the carrots and onions.

2 tbs. butter
6 medium carrots, peeled,
  thinly sliced
1 small onion, sliced
1 tsp. fresh ginger, grated
grated orange rind from 2 oranges

⅛ tsp. red pepper flakes
3 cups chicken stock
1½ cups fresh orange juice
salt and finely ground white pepper
grated carrot **or** thin orange slice for
  garnish

Melt butter over low heat in a large 3-quart saucepan. Add carrots, onions, ginger, orange rind and red pepper flakes. Cook over medium heat 4-5 minutes until onions begin to soften. Add chicken stock. Bring to a boil, cover and simmer about 35-40 minutes until carrots are tender. Remove from heat and let cool for a few minutes. Puree mixture in small batches in a food processor or blender. Add orange juice, salt and white pepper to taste. Serve hot or cold. If serving cold, chill in refrigerator several hours before serving. This soup freezes well.

Nutritional information per serving   120 calories, 5 grams fat, 3 grams saturated fat, 0 grams polyunsaturated fat, 1 gram monounsaturated fat, 4 grams protein, 16 grams carbohydrate, 11 mg cholesterol, 445 mg sodium

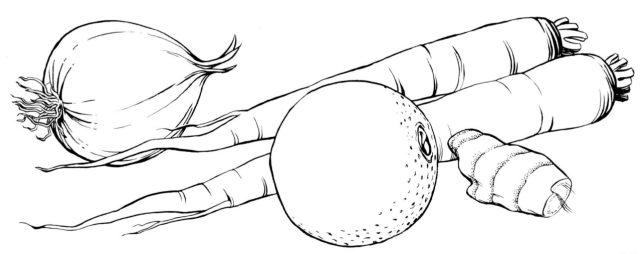

Gazpacho

Make this soup with ripe tomatoes for a summertime treat. It keeps well in the refrigerator for several days. The classic garnish of chopped onions, celery, green pepper and cucumber pieces have been put directly in the soup, so just add some fresh cilantro leaves when you pour it into a cup or dish.

¼ cup cider vinegar
1 cup fresh bread cubes
2 tsp. full-flavored olive oil
1 tbs. lemon juice
¼ tsp. cumin
1 large clove garlic, coarsely chopped
3 tbs. red onion, minced
3-4 medium ripe tomatoes, peeled, seeded, chopped with some juice
2 cups thick tomato juice
1 cup chicken stock
4 green onions, thinly sliced
⅓ cup celery, diced
3 tbs. green pepper, diced

3 tbs. pimiento, diced
½ cup cucumber, diced
salt and freshly ground pepper
fresh cilantro leaves for garnish

Soak fresh bread cubes in vinegar until soft. Place in blender with olive oil, lemon juice, cumin, garlic and 2 tbs. of red onion. Process until smooth. Pour into a large 1½-quart jar or bowl and add tomato pieces, tomato juice, chicken stock, remaining red onion, green onions, celery, green pepper, pimiento and cucumber pieces. Taste; add salt and pepper if needed. Refrigerate for several hours before serving. Add one or two ice cubes to your vacuum bottle to keep it nice and cold for lunch. Immediately before serving, garnish with fresh cilantro leaves.

Nutritional information per serving 110 calories, 3 grams fat, 1 gram saturated fat, .5 grams polyunsaturated fat, 2 grams monounsaturated fat, 4 grams protein, 18 grams carbohydrate, 0 mg cholesterol, 690+ mg sodium

Spicy Tomato Soup

This is the world's quickest soup. Carry the chicken and avocado pieces in a separate container with the fresh cilantro and add to the hot soup. It is also great served cold with the same garnishes. Add an ice cube or two to your vacuum bottle if you don't have a refrigerator.

1 (10 ozs.) can Snap-E-Tom Tomato and Chile Cocktail
2 tbs. avocado, diced
2 tbs. cooked chicken, diced
fresh cilantro leaves

Heat Snap-E-Tom cocktail in a microwavable bowl or cup. When hot add avocado and chicken pieces and float the fresh cilantro leaves on top. Serve with crisp pita or tortilla chips or bread sticks. Makes 1¼ cups.

Nutritional information per serving   160 calories, 9 grams fat, 2 grams saturated fat, 1 gram polyunsaturated fat, 5 grams monounsaturated fat, 8 grams protein, 17 grams carbohydrate, 13 mg cholesterol, 950 mg sodium

Be creative! Garnish with diced celery **or** green pepper and ham cubes.

Salads

Salads are a wonderful change of pace for the lunch box. They can be hearty when they include potatoes, pasta or beans, or lighter with simply marinated vegetables or lightly dressed greens. Crisp, colorful vegetables lightly dressed with a little good olive oil and a dash of one of the many aromatic vinegars or lemon juice provide some of the simplest and best salads.

Salads don't have to be the traditional tossed variety. Consider stuffing tomatoes, peppers or artichokes, or serving crisp vegetable sticks with a flavorful dip. Expand the fresh vegetable repertoire to include sugar snap or Chinese pea pods, jicama or fennel sticks, turnip or zucchini slices, cucumber sticks, different radish varieties, thin asparagus spears or green beans, green, red, yellow and black pepper strips, cauliflower and broccoli flowerettes. If the vegetables aren't tender, blanch them for a minute or two in boiling water and plunge them into cold water to refresh them. Keep two or three different flavors of vinegars on hand, and add a bottle of walnut, hazelnut or sesame oil to give your favorite salad dressing a new taste.

There are several ways to keep your salads cool until you are ready to eat them. One easy solution is to buy small blue ice packages, keep one or two in your freezer, and slip one in the bottom of your lunch bag, basket or insulated bag. Or freeze one of many flavors of fruit juices now available in small boxes, and use it for a lunch bag cooler. Insulated bags are available in many sizes, for a hot as well as a cold lunch. Double wrapping containers of cold salads in aluminum foil will also help keep things cool. Take the salad dressing in a separate little jar to pour over your salad just before eating. It is particularly important in the warm months to keep mayonnaise in salad dressings chilled. Commercial mayonnaise is less susceptible to spoilage if it gets warm than homemade mayonnaise, but care should be taken with any salad dressing containing uncooked eggs.

Basic Vinaigrette

Vary the ingredients in this basic recipe to create new tasting salad creations.

¼ cup full-flavored olive oil
1 tbs. red wine vinegar

⅛ tsp. sugar
salt and freshly ground pepper

Combine all ingredients in a small bowl or jar, mix well and toss with salad greens. Makes ¼ cup.

Nutritional information per tbs. 120 calories, 14 grams fat, 2 grams saturated fat, 1 gram polyunsaturated fat, 10 grams monounsaturated fat, 0 grams protein, 0 grams carbohydrate, 0 mg cholesterol, 0+ mg sodium

---

Be creative!
- Add ½ tsp. mustard.
- Substitute white wine vinegar with tarragon, sherry wine vinegar, rice wine vinegar or one of the wonderful fruit-flavored vinegars.
- Substitute walnut or hazelnut oil.
- Pour over warm cooked green beans or asparagus; sprinkle with chopped walnuts.

Tuscan Bean Salad

Servings: 4

Here is a hearty salad that is easy to put together from pantry ingredients. Use water pack tuna and the fat content is very low.

1 (15 ozs.) can cannellini beans
1 (6½ ozs.) can water pack tuna
2 tbs. celery, finely diced
2 tbs. red onion, finely diced
2 tbs. Italian parsley, minced
1 small clove garlic, minced
2 tbs. virgin olive oil

2 tbs. red wine vinegar
1 tbs. lemon juice
1 dash Tabasco sauce
salt and finely ground white pepper
fresh chopped tomato **or** roasted
   red pepper strips for garnish

Place beans in a sieve and rinse briefly under running water. Allow to drain. Add remaining ingredients to a bowl and stir with a fork to break up tuna pieces and combine ingredients. Add beans and mix gently. Best when refrigerated an hour or two before serving to allow flavors to marry. Garnish each serving with chopped tomato or strips of roasted red pepper.

Nutritional information per serving 250 calories, 7 grams fat, 1 gram saturated fat, 1 gram polyunsaturated fat, 5 grams monounsaturated fat, 20 grams protein, 27 grams carbohydrate, 23 mg cholesterol, 150+ mg sodium

Quick Corn Chowder (page 20) ▶

Mediterranean Salad

If you like eggplant, black olives and feta cheese, this recipe is for you. Eat as a salad, roll in crisp lettuce leaves or stuff a pita pocket. A microwave does a great job of cooking the eggplant with very little oil.

½ lb. small eggplant
1 tbs. full-flavored olive oil
1 large clove garlic, minced
¼ tsp. dried thyme, **or** a few
  sprigs of fresh
6-8 black Greek **or** Italian olives,
  pitted, coarsely chopped

2 ozs. feta cheese, crumbled
2 tbs. red onion, diced
¼ cup roasted red pepper, chopped
1 tbs. parsley, minced
1 tbs. lemon juice
freshly ground pepper

Cut unpeeled eggplants into ½" cubes. Place in a microwave dish with olive oil, minced garlic and thyme. Cover and cook on high power for 3 minutes. Stir, recover and cook for an additional 2 minutes. Let stand covered a few minutes before using. Makes approximately 1¾ cups diced eggplant. In a medium bowl combine remaining ingredients and cooked eggplant. Refrigerate for 1-2 hours before serving.

Nutritional information per serving 100 calories, 8 grams fat, 3 grams saturated fat, 1 gram polyunsaturated fat, 4 grams monounsaturated fat, 3 grams protein, 6 grams carbohydrate, 12 mg cholesterol, 225+ mg sodium

Savory Garbanzo and Artichoke Salad

Servings: 4

This quick salad features some wonderful Greek flavors. Serve with some Kalamata olives, cracker bread, and some crunchy carrot sticks or radishes and eat in a sunny picnic spot.

1 (15 ozs.) can garbanzo beans, drained, rinsed with cold water
1 (6½ ozs.) jar marinated artichoke crowns, drained, cut into ¾" chunks, reserve liquid
4-5 sun-dried tomatoes (packed in oil), cut into slivers
3 ozs. feta cheese, diced
2 green onions, thinly sliced
2 tbs. parsley, minced
¼ tsp. dried oregano
2 tbs. artichoke liquid
1 tbs. white wine vinegar
1 tsp. lemon juice
salt and freshly ground pepper

Combine all ingredients. Cover and refrigerate for 1-2 hours or overnight before serving.

Nutritional information per serving 260 calories, 11 grams fat, 4 grams saturated fat, 3 grams polyunsaturated fat, 2 grams monounsaturated fat, 13 grams protein, 33 grams carbohydrate, 19 mg cholesterol, 475+ mg sodium

Be creative!

- Add small cubes or slivers of salami to salad.
- Add peeled, seeded, chopped fresh tomato pieces to salad.
- Use salad for stuffing a tomato.

Deli Salad

The ingredients for this salad are cut in matchstick size. Use a coarse grating disk in the food processor for the pickle, apples and cheese. This dish is a good choice for a Dutch lunch or potluck, and keeps in the refrigerator for 2-3 days.

3 ozs. ham, **or** mortadella, **or**
    bologna (about 3 slices)
1 oz. salami (about 6 slices)
3 ozs. Gruyere **or** Swiss cheese
1 large dill **or** German style pickle
1 large **or** 2 small tart apples,
    peeled, cored

1 tbs. Worcestershire sauce
1 tbs. Dijon **or** stone ground mustard
1 tbs. reduced calorie mayonnaise
½ cup light sour cream
freshly ground pepper
2 tbs. parsley, minced

Cut ham, salami, cheese, pickle and apples into 1½"-2" long matchstick pieces. Cheese, pickle and apples can be grated with a coarse grating disk in the food processor. Place cut ingredients in a large mixing bowl. In a small bowl combine Worcestershire sauce, mustard, mayonnaise and sour cream. Blend well and pour over salad. Mix lightly with a fork and refrigerate 1-2 hours before serving. Serve in lettuce cups, pita pockets or cooked jumbo pasta shells.

Nutritional information per serving 275 calories, 21 grams fat, 12 grams saturated fat, 1 gram polyunsaturated fat, 6 grams monounsaturated fat, 11 grams protein, 11 grams carbohydrate, 41 mg cholesterol, 650+ mg sodium

Patio Salad

This hearty salad features pinto beans, yellow corn and green chilies for a south-of-the-border flavor. This is a good picnic side dish for barbecued steaks or chicken.

1 (15½ ozs.) can pinto beans,
    well drained
1 (12 ozs.) can whole kernel corn,
    well drained
1 cup cooked potatoes, diced
4-5 green onions, finely chopped
4-5 tbs. canned green chilies,
    finely chopped

½ tsp. chili powder
1 tsp. dried oregano
1 tsp. Dijon mustard
1 tbs. lemon juice
¼ cup reduced calorie mayonnaise
¼ cup light sour cream
2 tbs. parsley, minced
salt and freshly ground pepper

Rinse drained beans and corn under cold water and drain well. Place them in a large mixing bowl and add remaining ingredients. Gently mix with 2 forks. Chill in refrigerator for at least 2 hours before serving. This salad will keep, refrigerated, for 2-3 days.

Nutritional information per serving 175 calories, 4 grams fat, 2 grams saturated fat, 1 gram polyunsaturated fat, 1 gram monounsaturated fat, 2 grams protein, 29 grams carbohydrate, 2 mg cholesterol, 225+ mg sodium

Brown Rice Salad

The new low fat zesty smoked turkey sausage is great in this dish. Serve in a green or red pepper boat, a pita pocket or wrapped in a lettuce leaf.

2 cups cooked brown rice
½ cup low fat smoked turkey sausage, diced
⅓ cup carrot, coarsely grated
2 tbs. red onion, finely chopped
3 tbs. celery, finely chopped

3 tbs. sweet pickle, diced
2 tbs. parsley, minced
1 tbs. Dijon mustard
2 tbs. full-flavored olive oil
1 tbs. cider vinegar
salt and freshly ground pepper

Place all ingredients in a large glass or stainless mixing bowl and mix well. Cover and refrigerate for 1-2 hours before serving. This salad keeps well in the refrigerator for 2-3 days. If serving in a pepper boat, soften peppers either by parboiling for about 3 minutes or cook in a microwave.

Nutritional information per serving 280 calories, 13 grams fat, 3 grams saturated fat, 2 grams polyunsaturated fat, 7 grams monounsaturated fat, 9 grams protein, 35 grams carbohydrate, 24 mg cholesterol, 485+ mg sodium

Cold Shrimp and Noodle Salad

Servings: 6

Use thin Japanese or Chinese style noodles for this elegant salad. The vegetables should be cut in thin strips approximately the same diameter as the noodles.

8 ozs. fresh thin Oriental style noodles **or** 6 ozs. dry noodles
8 ozs. medium shrimp, cooked, peeled, deveined, **or** large salad shrimp
2 tbs. peanut oil
2 tbs. rice wine vinegar, **or** cider vinegar
1 tsp. sesame oil
1 tbs. light soy sauce
3-4 drops Tabasco
1 small carrot, coarsely grated **or** cut into thin strips
6-8 snow peas, blanched for 1 minute, cut into thin strips
3 green onions, white part only, cut into thin strips
salt and freshly ground pepper

Cook noodles according to package directions. Rinse under cold water and drain. Place in a large bowl and toss with peanut oil. Marinate shrimp in a small bowl with rice wine vinegar, sesame oil, soy sauce and Tabasco while preparing remaining ingredients. Add shrimp, carrot strips, snow peas and green onions to noodles. Toss with two forks. Chill for an hour in the refrigerator before serving.

Nutritional information per serving   140 calories, 6 grams fat, 1 gram saturated fat, 2 grams polyunsaturated fat, 3 grams monounsaturated fat, 10 grams protein, 11 grams carbohydrate, 85 mg cholesterol, 260+ mg sodium

Be creative!
- A lemon zester makes beautiful long thin carrot strips.
- Add bean sprouts.
- Add thin strips of fresh red or green pepper.

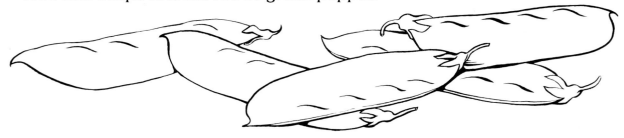

Confetti Pasta Salad

Crisp bits of fresh vegetables and cooked chicken make this a light pretty salad for year round enjoyment. Salad shrimp or ham chunks instead of chicken make for interesting variations.

4 ozs. dried corkscrew pasta
1 cup cooked chicken, diced
3 green onions, thinly sliced
½ medium sweet red **or** green pepper, diced
1 small carrot, coarsely grated
4-5 black olives, pitted, sliced
1 tbs. fresh sweet basil, minced **or**
   1 tsp. dried

2 tbs. Parmesan cheese, grated
red pepper flakes to taste
1 tsp. Dijon mustard
¼ cup full-flavored olive oil
1 tbs. white wine vinegar
1 tsp. lemon juice
salt and freshly ground pepper

Cook pasta according to package directions. Drain and rinse with cold water. Toss in a large bowl with 1 tbs. olive oil. Set aside to cool before adding other ingredients. Add onions, diced peppers, carrot, olives, sweet basil, Parmesan cheese and a dash of red pepper flakes. In a small bowl combine mustard, remaining olive oil, white wine vinegar and lemon juice. Mix well and beat to form an emulsion. Pour over pasta and vegetables and mix with 2 forks. Taste for seasoning; add salt and pepper to taste. Refrigerate before serving.

Nutritional information per serving 250 calories, 14 grams fat, 2 grams saturated fat, 1 gram polyunsaturated fat, 9 grams monounsaturated fat, 12 grams protein, 21 grams carbohydrate, 23 mg cholesterol, 110+ mg sodium

---

Dad's Favorite Marinated Cucumbers

2 cups

These crisp cucumbers and onions are great in pita pockets with grilled flank steak or chicken, or put them in an Armenian cracker bread roll. Start them a day before you want to use them so the flavors have time to blend. They keep well for 10 days in the refrigerator if they last that long.

1 medium (8 ozs.) cucumber **or**
  ½ European hothouse cucumber
½ large mild white onion
⅓ cup cider vinegar

½ tsp. salt
1 tsp. sugar
dash of Tabasco
water (about ⅔ cup)

Peel cucumber with a vegetable peeler and score lengthwise with tines of a fork to a depth of ⅛". Use the 2 mm slicer blade on the food processor or slice thinly by hand. Cut peeled onion in half and slice each half the same thickness as cucumbers. Place in a glass jar with a lid and add vinegar, salt, sugar and hot sauce. Shake well to mix. Add just enough water to cover. Allow to mellow in refrigerator for a day before serving.

Nutritional information per cup 25 calories, 0 grams fat, 0 grams saturated fat, 0 grams polyunsaturated fat, 0 grams monounsaturated fat, 1 gram protein, 7 grams carbohydrate, 0 mg cholesterol, 120 mg sodium

Garlicky Carrot Sticks

These are great to fill out the corners in the lunch box. Low calorie and slightly crunchy. They keep a week in the refrigerator.

3 large carrots, approx. ½ lb.
2 tbs. **Garlic-Flavored Olive Oil**, page 48

1 tbs. red wine vinegar
¼ tsp. dried oregano
salt and lots of freshly ground black pepper

Peel carrots and cut into 2"-long matchsticks. Cook carrots in a quart of rapidly boiling water 3-4 minutes. Carrots should be crisp tender. Drain and rinse with cold water. Place in a bowl and while still warm toss with olive oil, vinegar, oregano, salt and pepper. Remember to shake the bowl to distribute the marinade from time to time. Store in refrigerator. Recipe for **Garlic-Flavored Olive Oil** follows, but you can substitute a smashed clove of garlic and 2 tbs. of full-flavored olive oil. Remove garlic clove after a few hours. These would make a nice addition to an assortment of salads, or a sandwich accompaniment.

Nutritional information per serving 65 calories, 5 grams fat, 1 gram saturated fat, 0 grams polyunsaturated fat, 4 grams monounsaturated fat, 0 grams protein, 5 grams carbohydrate, 0 mg cholesterol, 15+ mg sodium

Marinated Asparagus Spears

Servings: 3

This salad features a light Oriental style marinade with a hint of orange. We like to peel the asparagus spears with a vegetable peeler because it makes the cooked asparagus very tender and easy to cut.

½ lb. asparagus, cooked
1 tbs. **Garlic-Flavored Olive Oil**, page 48
2 tsp. rice wine vinegar
1 tsp. sesame oil

1 tsp. soy sauce
1 tsp. orange juice
¼ tsp. sugar
salt and freshly ground pepper

Break heavy ends off asparagus and peel lower 2"-3" of stalk with a vegetable peeler. Cook until crisp tender, about 5-7 minutes, drain and cover with cold water. When cool, dry on paper towels. Place in a serving bowl or container. Combine **Garlic-Flavored Olive Oil**, rice wine vinegar, sesame oil, soy sauce, orange juice, sugar, salt and pepper to taste. Mix well and pour over asparagus. Coat asparagus with marinade. Serve immediately or cover and refrigerate for a few hours before serving. If you don't have **Garlic-Flavored Olive Oil** on hand, sauté 1 smashed clove of garlic in 1 tbs. olive oil for 2-3 minutes, discard garlic, and proceed with recipe.

Nutritional information per serving 90 calories, 7 grams fat, 1 gram saturated fat, 1 gram polyunsaturated fat, 5 grams monounsaturated fat, 2 grams protein, 5 grams carbohydrate, 0 mg cholesterol, 140+ mg sodium

---

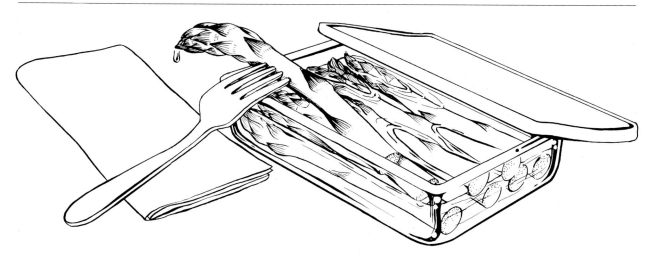

Garlic-Flavored Olive Oil

½ cup

This is a great all-purpose flavored olive oil. Use it in your marinated vegetables, brush it on pita chips with some fresh herbs, paint it on shrimps or vegetables for the barbecue, or make garlic bread or toasts.

½ cup light olive oil
⅛ tsp. red pepper flakes
6-8 garlic cloves, peeled, smashed

Heat olive oil, red pepper flakes and garlic cloves in a small heavy saucepan over very low heat for about 15 minutes, or until garlic is very lightly browned. Remove from heat and let garlic cool in oil. Strain and place in a small airtight jar for storage. This can be kept at room temperature.

Nutritional information per tbs. 125 calories, 14 grams fat, 2 grams saturated fat, 1 gram polyunsaturated fat, 10 grams monounsaturated fat, 0 grams protein. 1 gram carbohydrate, 0 mg cholesterol, 0 mg sodium

Cold Shrimp and Noodle Salad (page 40) ▶

New Potato Salad

Servings: 4

Use small new potatoes in their skins for this simple and quick salad.

12 ozs. small new potatoes
2 tbs. full-flavored olive oil
2 tsp. sherry wine vinegar **or** tarragon wine vinegar
salt and freshly ground black pepper
1 tsp. parsley, minced

Cook potatoes in water to cover for 20-25 minutes, just until firm, or cook in a microwave. When just cool enough to handle, slice each potato in about 4 slices. Place in a small bowl and gently toss with olive oil, vinegar, salt and pepper. Garnish with parsley.

Nutritional information per serving 170 calories, 8 grams fat, 1 gram saturated fat, 1 gram polyunsaturated fat, 6 grams monounsaturated fat, 2 grams protein, 24 grams carbohydrate, 0 mg cholesterol, 8+ mg sodium

Couscous Salad

Couscous, also called Moroccan pasta, is available in a quick cooking form that only takes five minutes to cook after the water boils. Here we pair it with some colorful fresh crunchy vegetables. This salad tastes even better the second day after it is made.

¾ cup water
1 tbs. olive oil
½ cup quick cooking couscous
¼ cup cucumber, diced
¼ cup carrot, coarsely grated
3-4 radishes, finely chopped
1 tbs. red onion, finely chopped
2 tbs. green pepper, finely chopped

2-3 black olives, chopped
1 tsp. capers
1 small tomato, peeled, seeded, chopped
1 tbs. Italian parsley, minced
salt and freshly ground pepper
1 tbs. full-flavored olive oil
2 tsp. balsamic vinegar

Bring water and 1 tbs. olive oil to a boil in a small saucepan. Add couscous, stir, cover and remove from heat. Let stand 5 minutes and then fluff with a fork. Set aside to let cool while preparing remaining ingredients. Place couscous in a medium sized bowl. Add chopped vegetables, salt, pepper, olive oil and balsamic vinegar. Use two forks to combine ingredients. Cover and refrigerate for several hours. This keeps well for 3-4 days in the refrigerator. Makes 3 cups.

Nutritional information per serving 185 calories, 12 grams fat, 2 grams saturated fat, 1 gram polyunsaturated fat, 9 grams monounsaturated fat, 3 grams protein, 18 grams carbohydrate, 0 mg cholesterol, 50+ mg sodium

---

Be creative! Serve in tomato or pepper cups.

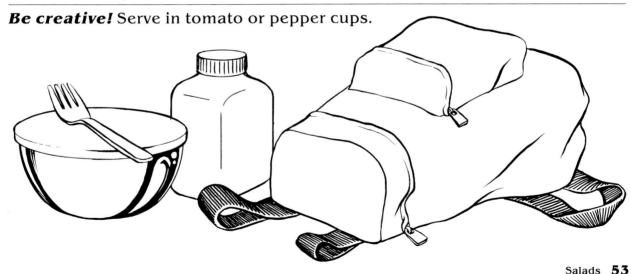

Orange and Fennel Salad

Thinly sliced oranges, some crunchy fennel and a dash of cumin make a very refreshing salad. Black olives make a striking garnish for this dish.

2 small oranges, **or** 1 large
1 piece of fennel, 2", cut into thin strips
1 small green onion, thinly sliced

⅛ tsp. cumin
½ tsp. light olive oil
salt and freshly ground pepper

Place the orange on a cutting board. Take a small sharp knife and cut off the peel, removing as much of the white membrane as possible. When peeled, cut in very thin round slices and place in a small bowl. Add diced fennel, sliced green onion, cumin, olive oil and black pepper. Cover and marinate in refrigerator for 1-2 hours before serving. This is a nice accompaniment to an assortment of salads or a slice of paté.

Nutritional information per serving 80 calories, 1 gram fat, 0 grams saturated fat, 0 grams polyunsaturated fat, 1 gram monounsaturated fat, 2 grams protein, 17 grams carbohydrate, 0 mg cholesterol, 8 mg sodium

---

Chicken and Turkey

Chicken and turkey are almost everyone's favorite meats because they are versatile, inexpensive, much lower in cholesterol than red meats, and easy to prepare. Cooked chicken or turkey are great in salads and sandwiches, so we have included easy recipes for poaching chicken breast halves or turkey tenderloins. You have an added bonus of some light homemade chicken stock for soups or sauces.

Baked and barbecued chicken pieces freeze beautifully and will defrost and be ready to eat in about 4 hours, keeping your lunch cool in the interim. **Chicken and Red Pepper Paté** can be served with crackers or spread on vegetables, or made into a sandwich. **Chinese Style Chicken Salad** makes zesty and delicious lunch box fare.

Perfect Poached Chicken Breasts

Servings: 2

Always tender and succulent, chicken breast meat has many uses. This is a master recipe that quickly produces cooked chicken with a minimum of work.

2 half breasts of chicken, about ¾-1 lb., **or** turkey, sliced into ½" thick slices
2-3 tbs. lemon juice
3-4 parsley sprigs
3-4 black peppercorns

Fill a large saucepan with 2 quarts of water. Add lemon juice, parsley sprigs and peppercorns. Cover pan and bring water to a rapid boil. Allow to boil for 2-3 minutes. Place chicken breasts in boiling water and immediately cover pot. Take off heat and let stand without lifting lid. In 18 minutes (for ¾ lbs. of chicken) or 20 minutes (for 1 lb. of chicken) remove chicken and plunge into a large bowl of very cold water to stop the cooking. Remove skin and bones. You will have approximately one half of the starting weight in delicious, moist, low fat chicken white meat. This is wonderful in chicken salads, sandwiches, stuffed avocadoes, etc.

Nutritional information per serving 300 calories, 8 grams fat, 2 grams saturated fat, 2 grams polyunsaturated fat, 3 grams monounsaturated fat, 57 grams protein, 0 grams carbohydrate, 152 mg cholesterol, 130+ mg sodium

Easy Barbecued Chicken

One or two pieces of this chicken can be frozen in a plastic bag for a quick lunch that will defrost by noon and keep the rest of the lunch box nice and cool.

2 lbs. chicken thighs, **or** chicken pieces of your choice
½ small onion, thinly sliced
¾ cup bottled barbecue sauce

Remove skin and put chicken, onions and barbecue sauce in a plastic food storage bag. Marinate about 30 minutes. Turn over once or twice so all pieces are coated with sauce. Preheat oven to 375°. Line a baking pan with aluminum foil. Place chicken and onions in pan and bake for 25 minutes, basting once or twice with barbecue sauce marinade. Turn chicken pieces over, increase oven heat to 400° and continue to bake for 20-25 minutes until chicken is done. Remove to a plate and let cool slightly before refrigerating or freezing.

This recipe can be made in a microwave in approximately 12 minutes but the appearance and texture are not as attractive as when baked in the oven.

Nutritional information per piece 190 calories, 6 grams fat, 1 gram saturated fat, 2 grams polyunsaturated fat, 2 grams monounsaturated fat, 28 grams protein, 5 grams carbohydrate, 114 mg cholesterol, 450 mg sodium

Orange Glazed Chicken Wings

Orange marmalade gives these chicken wings a rich brown glaze and a delicious flavor. These are fine at room temperature, or they can be refrigerated or frozen and popped into a microwave for a quick warm snack.

10 chicken wings
2 tbs. vegetable oil
¼ cup lite soy sauce
⅓ cup orange marmalade

1 tbs. cider vinegar
1 clove garlic, minced
⅛ tsp. hot pepper flakes

To prepare chicken wings, cut off wing tips and save for the stockpot. Cut through wing joint, separating wing into 2 parts. Cut off excess skin flaps. Combine remaining ingredients. Place wings in a food storage bag, pour marinade over them, close bag and refrigerate for several hours or overnight. Turn bag occasionally so all pieces receive some marinade. Preheat oven to 350°. Line a shallow pan with foil. Spray a baking rack with nonstick spray, or coat rack with oil. Arrange wings on rack, reserving marinade for basting. Bake for 25 minutes, basting once or twice, and turn over. Continue to bake for another 20-25 minutes until wings are done. Let cool 5 minutes before removing from rack. Serve warm or at room temperature. Refrigerate if not using in a short period of time.

__Nutritional information per piece__   78 calories, 5 grams fat, 1 gram saturated fat, 1 gram polyunsaturated fat, 2 grams monounsaturated fat, 5 grams protein, 4 grams carbohydrate, 14 mg cholesterol, 80 mg sodium

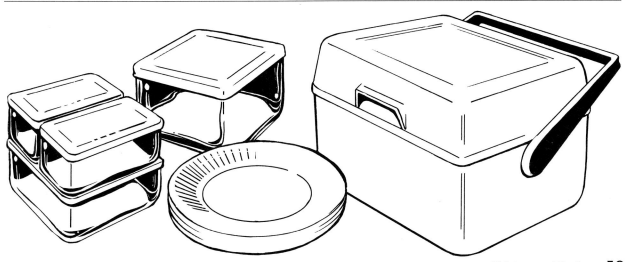

Honey Glazed Chicken Legs

Servings: 6

This is an easy baked chicken recipe using garlic, ginger and honey to give the chicken pieces a little lift. Marinate them for several hours or overnight.

6 thighs and 6 drumsticks
½ cup lite soy sauce
⅓ cup honey

2 tbs. vegetable oil
1 clove garlic, minced
1 tsp. fresh ginger, grated

Remove skin from chicken pieces and cut off excess fat. Combine remaining ingredients and place with chicken in a food storage bag placed in a low bowl. Close bag and refrigerate for several hours or overnight, turning the bag occasionally so all the pieces are covered by the marinade. Preheat oven to 375°. Line a jelly roll pan or shallow baking pan with foil. Remove chicken pieces from marinade and place on foil. Discard marinade. Bake for 25 minutes. Turn chicken pieces over and increase oven temperature to 400°. Continue to bake for 20-25 minutes until chicken is done. Remove to a plate and let cool slightly before refrigerating or freezing.

Nutritional information per serving 300 calories, 14 grams fat, 3 grams saturated fat, 4 grams polyunsaturated fat, 5 grams monounsaturated fat, 29 grams protein, 17 grams carbohydrate, 116 mg cholesterol, 600 mg sodium

Chicken and Red Pepper Paté

This paté doesn't require any cooking if you have some leftover chicken on hand. Spread on crackers or use for stuffing for small hard rolls or fresh whole peppers. This mixture is also stiff enough to mold. Choose a small round bowl, or form into a log about 2" in diameter and roll up in waxed paper. Refrigerate until ready to use.

2 cups cooked chicken, coarsely chopped
4 ozs. light cream cheese
1 tsp. Dijon mustard
3 green onions, minced

2 tbs. parsley, minced
¼ tsp. dried thyme
salt and freshly ground pepper
3 tbs. roasted red pepper, chopped
parsley sprigs for garnish

Place chicken in food processor bowl with cream cheese and mustard. Process until smooth. Add onions, parsley, thyme, salt and pepper, and pulse 3 or 4 times to combine. Remove from bowl and stir in chopped red peppers. Place in mold or form into a log, cover and refrigerate until ready to serve. Garnish with minced parsley, and use a small knife for a spreader.

Nutritional information per serving   225 calories, 15 grams fat, 8 grams saturated fat, 1 gram polyunsaturated fat, 5 grams monounsaturated fat, 21 grams protein, 2 grams carbohydrate, 90 mg cholesterol, 150+ mg sodium

Chinese Style Chicken Salad

Servings: 2

Take the lettuce, grated carrot and green onions in one plastic container and the marinated chicken in another. Combine them when you are ready to eat.

1 cup cooked chicken pieces,
   shredded **or** cut into slivers
1 tbs. lite soy sauce
1 tbs. rice wine vinegar
1 tbs. peanut oil
1 tsp. sesame oil
2 tsp. Dijon mustard
dash red pepper flakes

¼ tsp. sugar
salt and freshly ground pepper
1½ cups iceberg lettuce, shredded
1 cup carrot, coarsely grated
2 green onions, thinly sliced
2 tbs. dry roasted unsalted peanuts,
   coarsely chopped
fresh cilantro leaves for garnish

Combine shredded chicken, soy sauce, rice wine vinegar, peanut oil, sesame oil, mustard, red pepper flakes, sugar, salt and pepper in a small bowl or plastic bag. Let chicken marinate while preparing remaining ingredients, or for several hours in the refrigerator. To assemble, shred lettuce and carrots and place on plate or platter. Sprinkle with green onion slices. Drizzle marinade from chicken over lettuce and carrot. Mound chicken in center and garnish with peanuts and fresh cilantro leaves.

***Nutritional information per serving** 300 calories, 19 grams fat, 3 grams saturated fat, 6 grams polyunsaturated fat, 8 grams monounsaturated fat, 23 grams protein, 11 grams carbohydrate, 58 mg cholesterol, 450+ mg sodium*

Fish

Nutritious and flavorful, fish is an excellent addition to the lunch box. The small cooked salad shrimp are all ready to go. Dress them with a little light mayonnaise or herbed vinaigrette and roll up in a lettuce leaf. It just takes a few minutes to cook the vegetables for **Caponata** in a microwave; add a can of tuna, and you have a pretty, delicious fish salad to eat on crackers or in a lettuce cup. **Tuna Mayonnaise** is very versatile and is as good on cooked vegetables as it is on chicken or pork. The piquant, sweet sour **West Indian Marinated Fish** is one of those dishes that taste better the next day when the flavors have had a chance to combine. The recipe for **Perfect Poached Fish** can be used for salmon, halibut, red snapper and other firm-fleshed fish. Break away from tuna sandwiches and try some of these fish ideas.

Perfect Poached Salmon Steaks

Servings: 2

Light, full of flavor and very easy to prepare, a piece of poached salmon makes a wonderful lunch. Accompany with a lightly dressed salad and buttered whole wheat bread.

2 salmon steaks, about 8 ozs. each
2 tbs. lemon juice
3-4 parsley sprigs

3-4 whole black peppercorns
½ cup dry white wine

Put a large saucepan containing 2 quarts of water, lemon juice, parsley, peppercorns and white wine over high heat, cover and bring to a rapid boil. Allow to boil for 2-3 minutes. Gently lower steaks into boiling liquid and immediately recover pan. Take off heat and let stand for 10 minutes. Carefully lift out fish with a slotted spoon and place on a plate to cool. Cover and refrigerate when cool.

Nutritional information per serving   400 calories, 24 grams fat, 6 grams saturated fat, 5 grams polyunsaturated fat, 10 grams monounsaturated fat, 45 grams protein, 0 grams carbohydrate, 150 mg cholesterol, 110+ mg sodium

Marinated Shrimp

Several of these mildly piquant shrimp topping a green salad make a delicious lunch, or add them to sliced tomatoes and olives.

½ lb. medium sized shrimp,
  peeled, deveined
1 tbs. parsley, chopped
1 tbs. full-flavored olive oil
1 tbs. tarragon wine vinegar

1 tbs. lemon juice
1 tsp. Dijon mustard
3-4 drops Tabasco
2 green onions, finely chopped
salt and freshly ground pepper

Cook shrimp in boiling salted water for about 1 minute or until they turn pink and are just firm. Drain well. Combine remaining ingredients and pour over shrimp while still warm. Mix well. Cover and refrigerate for 3-4 hours before serving. These can be made a day ahead.

Nutritional information per serving 110 calories, 5 grams fat, 1 gram saturated fat, 1 gram polyunsaturated fat, 3 grams monounsaturated fat, 13 grams protein, 2 grams carbohydrate, 100 mg cholesterol, 115+ mg sodium

**Alternatives to Bread (page 10),
Stuffed Jumbo Shells (page 82), Lunch Kebobs (page 9),
Vegetable Sandwich Spread (page 114) and Sandwich Combinations (page 103)** ▶

Creamy Shrimp Spread

This mixture makes a great stuffing for cooked artichokes, or use it as a dip with sliced vegetables or pita chips.

3 ozs. small, cooked salad shrimp
2 tbs. low calorie mayonnaise
2 tbs. light sour cream
cayenne pepper

If shrimp are quite large, cut them in half. Combine shrimp, mayonnaise, sour cream and a couple of dashes of cayenne. If using as a stuffing for artichokes, remove the center choke and fill with shrimp mixture. Makes filling for 3 medium sized artichokes.

Nutritional information per serving 75 calories, 4 grams fat, 2 grams saturated fat, 1 gram polyunsaturated fat, 1 gram monounsaturated fat, 7 grams protein, 2 grams carbohydrate, 52 mg cholesterol, 110 mg sodium

Be creative! Use 1 tbs. low calorie mayonnaise and 1 tbs. light sour cream with 2 tbs. celery. Serve on cucumber, jicama or turnip slices, tortilla chips or as a filling for lightly blanched snow pea pods opened up to make little boats.

◀ **Guacamole Dip (page 95)**   Fish **69**

Seviche

This tangy lemon-and-lime marinated fish makes a great summer lunch dish. The fish is "cooked" by the acid in the citrus juice, not by heat. Don't skimp on the avocado and tomato pieces. Serve in a lettuce cup with some crisp tortilla chips or crackers.

½ lb. fresh sole filets
2 tbs. lemon juice
1 tbs. lime juice
1 tbs. canned green chilies, chopped
1 tbs. pimiento pieces, chopped
1 tsp. prepared salsa, hot **or**
    medium intensity

2 tsp. olive oil
⅛ tsp. oregano
salt and freshly ground pepper
1 small avocado, diced
1 small tomato, peeled, seeded,
    chopped
fresh cilantro leaves for garnish

Cut fish into ½"-¾" pieces. Cover with lemon and lime juices and marinate for several hours, or overnight. Fish will become opaque and take on a "cooked" appearance and texture. Drain well, discard lemon-lime mixture, place in a serving container and add green chilies, pimiento, salsa, olive oil, oregano, salt and pepper. Mix well. Just before serving add diced avocado, tomato and cilantro leaves. Refrigerate until ready to serve.

Nutritional information per serving 190 calories, 14 grams fat, 2 grams saturated fat, 2 grams polyunsaturated fat, 8 grams monounsaturated fat, 12 grams protein, 7 grams carbohydrate, 33 mg cholesterol, 50+ mg sodium

Be creative! Use ½ lb. tiny bay scallops in place of sole.

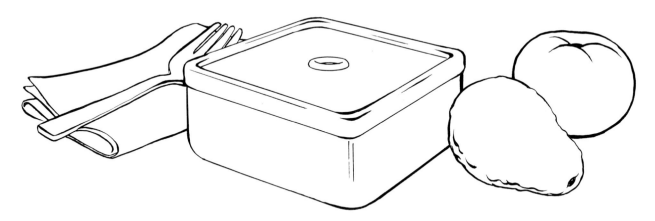

Smoked Salmon and Dilled Potato Salad Servings: 4

New potatoes in their skins and just a little smoked salmon make an elegant different salad.

12 ozs. small new potatoes, unpeeled
1 tbs. sweet hot mustard
1 tbs. lowfat yogurt
¼ tsp. dried dill, **or** 2 tsp. fresh dill, chopped
1 tsp. parsley, minced
salt and freshly ground pepper
1-2 ozs. thinly sliced smoked salmon, cut into 1" squares

Cook potatoes in boiling water for 20-25 minutes, or until just tender. When cool enough to handle, slice each potato in quarters and place in a bowl. Mix together sweet hot mustard, yogurt, dill and parsley and gently toss with potatoes. Season with salt and pepper to taste. Add smoked salmon pieces and mix gently. This can be made a day ahead. Refrigerate until ready to serve. Makes about 2½ cups.

Nutritional information per serving 110 calories, 1 gram fat, 0 grams saturated fat, 0 grams polyunsaturated fat, 0 grams monounsaturated fat, 4 grams protein, 21 grams carbohydrate, 3 mg cholesterol, 150+ mg sodium

Tuna Mayonnaise

This is a basic mayonnaise that transforms cooked chicken, turkey or pork into something very special. It is also delicious on cooked sliced new potatoes or cooked green beans.

1 whole egg
1 tbs. lemon juice
salt and finely ground white pepper
¾ cup light olive oil **or** peanut oil
dash of Tabasco

1 tsp. anchovy paste
1 (3½ ozs.) can Italian style tuna
  with oil
black olives and roasted red pepper
  strips for garnish

Place egg, lemon juice, salt and pepper in blender or food processor bowl. Blend for a few seconds. With motor running, slowly add oil until mixture thickens. Add Tabasco, anchovy paste and tuna with oil. Continue to blend until mixture is smooth. Combine 1 cup cooked chicken, turkey or pork pieces with ¼ cup of tuna mayonnaise. Garnish with black olives and red pepper strips and serve in tomato cups, blanched red or green pepper boats or in a pita pocket.

Nutritional information per tbs. 90 calories, 10 grams fat, 3 grams saturated fat, 2 grams polyunsaturated fat, 13 grams monounsaturated fat, 1 gram protein, 0 grams carbohydrate, 11 mg cholesterol, 50+ mg sodium

West Indian Marinated Fish

This is another dish that is better the next day. Use a firm-fleshed fish such as red snapper, halibut, orange roughy or sea bass. Serve as one selection on a plate of salads, or alone with some crisp breadsticks or cracker bread.

1 lb. fresh red snapper fillets
flour seasoned with salt and
   freshly ground pepper
¼ cup peanut oil
2 tbs. full-flavored olive oil
1 medium onion, thinly sliced
3 cloves garlic, peeled, smashed
1 small carrot, thinly sliced
½ cup cider vinegar

¼ cup water
1 tsp. brown sugar
1 tbs. lemon juice
salt and freshly ground pepper
dash red pepper flakes
½ tsp. dried thyme, **or** 2 sprigs fresh
2 tbs. white raisins
1 tbs. capers
black olives for garnish

Cut each fish fillet into 2-3 medium pieces. Dredge in seasoned flour. Heat peanut oil in a large skillet. When hot quickly sauté fish 3-4 minutes on each side, until done. Remove fish and place in one layer in a deep-sided glass or stainless steel dish (not aluminum). Discard oil, wipe out pan, add olive oil to pan and heat over medium heat. Add sliced onion, carrots and garlic cloves. Cook 2-3 minutes until onion and carrot soften. Add vinegar, water, brown sugar, lemon juice, salt and pepper, red pepper flakes, thyme and raisins to skillet. Bring to a boil and boil 2-3 minutes. Pour over fish. Sprinkle on raisins and capers, cool to room temperature, and then cover and refrigerate. Serve at room temperature.

Nutritional information per serving   240 calories, 12 grams fat, 2 grams saturated fat, 2 grams polyunsaturated fat, 7 grams monounsaturated fat, 24 grams protein, 10 grams carbohydrate, 42 mg cholesterol, 120 mg sodium

Be creative! Substitute red pepper strips and pine nuts for carrots and raisins.

Caponata

Caponata originated in Sicily and is generally considered a relish because of its sweet and sour flavors. This is very easy to do in a microwave. The vegetables cook perfectly and retain their brilliant colors. Mix with a can of albacore tuna and you have a wonderful Dutch lunch or antipasto. Serve with crisp crackerbread, or roll in a lettuce leaf, or tuck into a pita pocket.

2 tbs. full-flavored olive oil
½ lb. eggplant, peeled, cut into ½" cubes
½ medium onion, chopped
3 cloves garlic, smashed
⅓ cup celery, thinly sliced
½ medium green pepper, peeled,
　cut into ¾" squares
½ red pepper, peeled, cut into ¾" squares
½ cup carrots, thinly sliced

2 medium tomatoes, peeled,
　seeded, chopped
½ tsp. sugar
2 tbs. red wine vinegar
salt and freshly ground pepper
1 tbs. capers
1 (6½ ozs.) can tuna fish,
　packed in water
8-10 black olives for garnish

Place oil in a 2-quart microwave dish with cover. Add eggplant and stir to coat with oil. Cover and microwave on high 3 minutes. Add onion, garlic, celery, green and red pepper squares, carrots and tomatoes. Dissolve sugar in red wine vinegar. Add to vegetables; cover and cook on high for 3 minutes. Remove and let stand covered for 2 minutes. When cool add salt, pepper, capers, drained tuna fish and black olives. This will keep for several days in the refrigerator. Serve at room temperature.

Nutritional information per serving 186 calories, 10 grams fat, 1 gram saturated fat, 1 gram polyunsaturated fat, 7 grams monounsaturated fat, 14 grams protein, 13 grams carbohydrate, 23 mg cholesterol, 250+ mg sodium

Snacks

Here is a collection of snack ideas for the times you want something lighter or when several of you are sharing lunches. Finger foods, vegetable dips, stuffed ham, beef or turkey rolls, filled jumbo pasta shells, Greek style dolmas and marinated mushrooms are some ways to brighten the lunch box menu. Snacks can be added to the heartier eater's lunch box to provide extra energy for the working man or growing boy. Many of these recipes can be made for a single serving or multiplied to fit the crowd. Stash some of these snacks in the refrigerator to bring out when you issue a last minute invitation to friends to stop by for a glass of wine.

Ham Pinwheels

These attractive nibbles are easy to make ahead. Substitute canned green chili strips for a taste variation, or do some of each for a colorful plate.

1 (4 ozs.) pkg. Danish ham (5 slices)
4 ozs. light cream cheese
1 (7 ozs.) jar roasted red peppers

Pat each slice of ham dry on paper towels. Thinly spread with cream cheese. Pat peppers dry on paper towels and cut into 3/8" wide strips. Place a strip of pepper along a narrow side of the ham slice, and then 4-5 more strips parallel to the first one, spaced at ¾" intervals. Leave a ¾" border at the top. Roll into a tight roll and refrigerate for at least an hour to firm. Just before serving, cut each roll into 5 pieces, and arrange so that "pretty side" is up.

Nutritional information per piece 24 calories, 2 grams fat, 1 gram saturated fat, .5 grams polyunsaturated fat, .5 grams monounsaturated fat, 2 grams protein, 1 gram carbohydrate, 7 mg cholesterol, 80 mg sodium

---

Dolmas

Stuffed grape leaves make wonderful additions to the lunch box or the appetizer tray. They keep well in the refrigerator for several days.

¼ cup olive oil
1 large onion, chopped
1 clove garlic, minced
salt and freshly ground pepper
½ cup uncooked rice
½ tsp. dill weed
3 tbs. parsley, minced
2 tbs. almonds **or** pine nuts

¼ cup lemon juice
½ cup water
3 tbs. olive oil
½ lb. mushrooms, finely chopped
1 (8 ozs.) jar grape leaves in brine
2 tbs. olive oil
2 tbs. lemon juice
1½ cups chicken stock **or** water

Heat ¼ cup olive oil in a large skillet. Add chopped onion and garlic and sauté until tender but not browned. Add salt, pepper and rice to onions. Cook slowly 10 minutes, stirring frequently. Add dill, parsley, nuts, lemon juice and water. Stir well. Cover and simmer gently until liquid has been absorbed, approximately 15-20 minutes. Heat 3 tbs. olive oil in another small skillet. Sauté chopped mushrooms for 3-4 minutes until mixture is fairly dry. Add to rice mixture after rice has cooked. Rinse grape leaves under running water. Separate, and trim long stems flush at top of leaf. Place leaves shiny side down on a plate or board. To fill, place 1 teaspoon of rice-mushroom mixture near the stem end and roll up jelly roll fashion, tucking in sides of leaves to make a neat package as you roll. Place stuffed leaves in a skillet large enough to hold them in one layer. Pour in olive oil, lemon juice and water or chicken stock. There should be enough liquid in pan to come half-way up sides of dolmas. Place a large flat lid or plate directly on top of rolls. Cover pan with foil or another lid. Simmer 35 minutes. Add more liquid during cooking if necessary. Remove to a platter and cool.

Nutritional information per dolma   40 calories, 3 grams fat, 0 grams saturated fat, 0 grams polyunsaturated fat, 2 grams monounsaturated fat, 1 gram protein, 4 grams carbohydrate, 0 mg cholesterol, 1+ mg sodium

Stuffed Jumbo Shells

Stuffed jumbo pasta shells make a great snack for the lunch box or substantial appetizers. Some hot and cold filling recipes follow.

Basic cooking and filling instructions: cook jumbo pasta shells in approximately 4 quarts of boiling water according to the package directions. The shells should keep their shape and be cooked but a little firm, so test them at the shorter cooking time. Drain and rinse the cooked shells under cold water for easier handling. Set aside until ready to be filled. Shells will wait at room temperature until you are ready to stuff them. Cooked jumbo shells hold approximately 2 tablespoons of filling, and are easy to fill with a teaspoon.

These fillings can be used to stuff a hollowed out hard roll or parboiled peppers and reheated in a microwave.

Jumbo Tuna and Cheddar Shells

These tasty tuna treats melt in your mouth. Accompany with ripe cherry tomatoes, sweet pickle chunks and some good black olives.

8 jumbo pasta shells, cooked
1 tbs. butter
¼ cup onion, finely chopped
1 (6½ ozs.) can water packed tuna, drained
2 ozs. light cream cheese, softened

½ cup sharp cheddar cheese, coarsely grated
2 tbs. pimientos **or** roasted red peppers, chopped
freshly ground pepper

Melt butter in a small nonstick skillet. Sauté onions over low heat 4-5 minutes until soft. In a small bowl combine onions, tuna and cream cheese and blend well. Add grated cheddar, chopped pimiento and freshly ground pepper. Mixture will be fairly stiff. Stuff each shell with about 2 tbs. of filling and refrigerate until ready to serve. These keep in the refrigerator for 2-3 days. Reheat in a microwave covered with plastic wrap. Serve warm.

Nutritional information per shell   120 calories, 6 grams fat, 4 grams saturated fat, 0 grams polyunsaturated fat, 2 grams monounsaturated fat, 9 grams protein, 6 grams carbohydrate, 30 mg cholesterol, 150+ mg sodium

Spinach and Clam Shells

Spinach, clams and garlic are a classic combination. If you use frozen spinach be sure to drain well and squeeze as dry as possible.

10 jumbo pasta shells, cooked
2 tsp. butter
¼ cup onion, finely chopped
2 cloves garlic, minced
½ cup spinach, cooked, finely chopped
(about ½ of a 10 oz. pkg.)

¾ cup ricotta cheese
2 (6½ ozs.) cans chopped clams, drained
3 tbs. Parmesan cheese, grated
salt and freshly ground pepper

Melt butter in a small nonstick skillet. Sauté onions over low heat 4-5 minutes. When onion is almost soft, add garlic and cook for another minute. In a medium sized bowl combine onion, garlic, spinach, ricotta cheese, drained clams, 2 tbs. of Parmesan cheese, salt and pepper. Mix well. Stuff shells and sprinkle with remaining 1 tbs. Parmesan cheese. Refrigerate until ready to serve. These may be refrigerated for 2-3 days. Reheat in a microwave covered with plastic wrap. Serve warm.

Nutritional information per shell 100 calories, 3 grams fat, 2 grams saturated fat, 0 grams polyunsaturated fat, 1 gram monounsaturated fat, 10 grams protein, 7 grams carbohydrate, 26 mg cholesterol, 95+ mg sodium

Spicy Chicken Shells

These go together very quickly if you have some leftover roast chicken. Serve cold with crisp tortilla chips and cherry tomatoes.

8 jumbo pasta shells, cooked
2 ozs. light cream cheese
¼ cup prepared chunky salsa,
  hot or mild
1 tbs. fresh cilantro, chopped

2 tbs. almonds, toasted,
  coarsely chopped
1 cup cooked chicken, diced
salt and freshly ground pepper
fresh cilantro leaves for garnish

In a medium sized bowl combine cream cheese, salsa, chopped cilantro and almonds. Mix well. Add chicken pieces. Stuff cooked pasta shells and garnish each shell with a fresh whole cilantro leaf. Refrigerate. Remove from refrigerator about 15 minutes before serving to bring out the flavors.

Nutritional information per shell 95 calories, 5 grams fat, 2 grams saturated fat, 1 gram polyunsaturated fat, 2 grams monounsaturated fat, 7 grams protein, 6 grams carbohydrate, 22 mg cholesterol, 40+ mg sodium

Be creative!
- Use filling to stuff perfect ripe tomatoes.
- Use as a filling for pita pockets and add a small piece of lettuce for crunch.
- Wrap filling in a crisp lettuce leaf.

Shrimp Salad Shells

This low calorie shrimp salad also is great rolled in a lettuce leaf, on crackers or tortilla chips, or as a stuffing for cherry tomatoes.

6 jumbo pasta shells, cooked
2 green onions, thinly sliced
2 tbs. celery, finely diced
2 tbs. parsley, finely minced
1 tsp. lemon juice
1 tbs. reduced calorie mayonnaise
7 ozs. small cooked salad shrimp
salt and finely ground white pepper

Combine all ingredients and mix lightly with a fork. If shrimp are 1"-1½" in size, cut each in half. Fill pasta shells using a small spoon and refrigerate until ready to serve. These are best when used within a day of making.

Nutritional information per shell   70 calories, 1 gram fat, 0 grams saturated fat, 1 gram polyunsaturated fat, 0 grams monounsaturated fat, 8 grams protein, 6 grams carbohydrate, 50 mg cholesterol, 65+ mg sodium

Deviled Eggs

Be creative! Add these combinations to cooked egg yolks:

- smoked salmon, fresh **or** dried dill weed and mayonnaise
- sardines, mustard and mayonnaise
- pesto and light cream cheese
- olive paste and light sour cream
- cooked shrimp **or** chicken with curry powder, chutney and light sour cream
- chopped, stuffed green olives and mayonnaise
- prepared salsa, hot **or** mild, and light sour cream
- cooked asparagus, Danish ham and mayonnaise . . . save an asparagus tip or two for garnishing the top
- cooked mushrooms, tarragon and light sour cream
- cooked tiny peas, green onions and mayonnaise
- ham with dill pickle, mustard and mayonnaise
- capers, pine nuts and mayonnaise

Hummus bi Tahini

Use crisp raw vegetable slices or pieces of cracker bread to scoop up this popular Middle Eastern dip. We prefer to use the Oriental style sesame paste. It is made from toasted sesame seeds and has more character than the traditional tahini.

2 cloves garlic
1 (15½ ozs.) can garbanzo beans
¼ cup Oriental sesame paste
1 tbs. full-flavored olive oil
⅓ cup lemon juice

1 tsp. cumin
salt and finely ground white pepper
paprika, fresh cilantro, and
    black olives **or** cherry tomato
    halves for garnish

In a food processor with motor running, drop garlic cloves into feed tube. Drain garbanzo beans, reserving about 3 tbs. of the liquid. Place garbanzo beans in food processor bowl with 2 tbs. of liquid, sesame paste, olive oil and lemon juice. Process until smooth. Scrape down container sides and add cumin, salt and pepper. Process for another few seconds to mix. If mixture seems too thick to dip, add remaining tbs. of garbanzo liquid, or water. Pour into a serving container or dish and sprinkle lightly with paprika. Refrigerate or set in a cool place for an hour or two for flavors to develop. Garnish with fresh cilantro leaves and black olives, or cherry tomato halves. Use an assortment of fresh vegetable pieces such as carrots, blanched snow peas, zucchini, cucumber, red and green peppers, fennel, jicama, turnips and cracker bread or toasted pita chips for dipping. This keeps well for several days in the refrigerator.

Nutritional information per ¼ cup   165 calories, 8 grams fat, 1 gram saturated fat, 3 grams polyunsaturated fat, 4 grams monounsaturated fat, 7 grams protein, 18 grams carbohydrate, 0 mg cholesterol, 6+ mg sodium

Crisp Pita Chips

These are easy to make and are a great lowfat, low sodium substitute for potato or tortilla chips or crackers. Use with dips or cheese or eat with soup. Make a couple of cookie sheets full, about half a large package of pita bread at a time. They keep well in an airtight container.

1 pita bread, 6"

Preheat oven to 200°. Cut pita bread into 8 wedges. Take each wedge apart and place triangles on a cookie sheet, center side up. Bake at 200°-225° for about 30 minutes until crisp and dry, but not brown. Let cool and store in an airtight container. You can bake these at a higher temperature, but be sure to watch them. They brown very easily. Baking at 300° takes approximately 10 minutes.

Nutritional information per chip   10 calories, 0 grams fat, 0 grams saturated fat, 0 grams polyunsaturated fat, 0 grams monounsaturated fat, 0 grams protein, 2 grams carbohydrate, 0 mg cholesterol, 20 mg sodium

---

Be creative!

- Take whole pita breads apart before cutting. Lightly brush with olive oil and sprinkle with Parmesan cheese or dried herbs before baking.
- Cut pita bread into wedges, spread insides with black olive paste and bake as above.
- Cut pita bread into wedges and place thin slices of cheese, cut to the same shape, inside. Just before eating, microwave briefly to melt cheese.

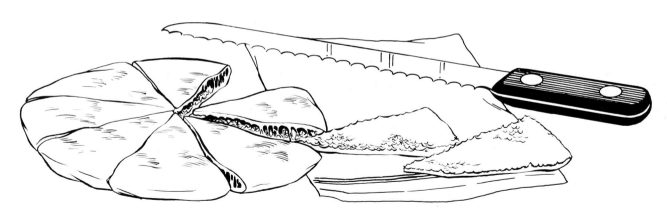

Marinated Mushrooms

These appetizing mushrooms keep very well in the refrigerator for a week and are good low calorie corner fillers in the lunch box. They make a great quick bite to keep the wolf away before dinner.

½ lb. small button mushrooms
¼ cup **Garlic-Flavored Olive Oil**, page 48
¼ cup rice wine vinegar
⅛ tsp. red pepper flakes

1 tbs. lemon juice
¼ tsp. sugar
½ tsp. thyme
½ tsp. sweet basil
salt and freshly ground pepper

If you don't have **Garlic-Flavored Olive Oil**, use 1 clove of smashed garlic and ¼ cup olive oil. Place in a small saucepan with rice wine vinegar, red pepper flakes, lemon juice, sugar, thyme, sweet basil, salt and pepper. Bring to a boil over medium heat; reduce heat and simmer for 5 minutes. Trim stems off mushrooms. If mushrooms are large, cut them into quarters; if small just trim caps; place in saucepan with olive oil and vinegar mixture. Simmer for 5 minutes. Remove from heat and let mushrooms cool in marinade. Put mushrooms into a small jar, pour marinade over and cover tightly. Refrigerate until ready to use. These keep well for about a week.

Nutritional information per ¼ cup (drained)   60 calories, 6 grams fat, 1 gram saturated fat, 1 gram polyunsaturated fat, 4 grams monounsaturated fat, 2 grams protein, 6 grams carbohydrate, 0 mg cholesterol, 5+ mg sodium

---

Asparagus Ham Rolls

Take one medium spear of tender crisp cooked asparagus and wrap it in a small strip of ham coated with a soy- or orange-flavored light cream cheese and you have a delicious snack for lunch.

8 asparagus spears, cooked tender crisp
1 tbs. light cream cheese
½ tsp. light soy sauce
2 rectangular slices of Danish ham, 6" each

Soften cream cheese by beating with soy sauce. Spread a thin layer on each ham slice. Cut ham slice into 4 rectangles. Roll each rectangle around 1 asparagus spear. Eat with fingers.

Nutritional information per roll 18 calories, 1 gram fat, 1 gram saturated fat, 0 grams polyunsaturated fat, 0 grams monounsaturated fat, 2 grams protein, 1 gram carbohydrate, 5 mg cholesterol, 110 mg sodium

Be creative! Use ½ tsp. orange juice and a little grated orange rind with the light cream cheese instead of soy sauce.

Curried Egg Dip

¾ cup

Hard-boiled eggs are complemented with a touch of curry. This is great with crisp vegetable sticks or pita chips.

⅔ cup light sour cream
½ tsp. curry powder
½ tsp. Dijon mustard

salt and freshly ground pepper
1 hard-boiled egg, finely chopped

Combine ingredients, mix well and refrigerate for 2-3 hours before serving.

Nutritional information per ¼ cup 95 calories, 8 grams fat, 5 grams saturated fat, 1 gram polyunsaturated fat, 3 grams monounsaturated fat, 4 grams protein, 3 grams carbohydrate, 90 mg cholesterol, 55+ mg sodium

Guacamole Dip

1½ cups

Try this light south-of-the-border dip.

1 large ripe avocado
1 green onion, chopped
2 tbs. fresh lime juice

½ cup plain nonfat yogurt
¼ tsp. garlic salt
3 drops Tabasco

Combine ingredients, mix well and refrigerate for 2-3 hours before serving.

Nutritional information per 3 tbs. 64 calories, 5 grams fat, 1 gram saturated fat, 1 gram polyunsaturated fat, 3 grams monounsaturated fat, 2 grams protein, 4 grams carbohydrate, 1 mg cholesterol, 84 mg sodium

Vegetable Dip

This is a thick delicious dip with chopped artichoke crowns and fresh tomato pieces. Carrot and fennel sticks, tortilla chips and rye crisp make great dippers.

⅓ cup lowfat yogurt
⅓ cup ricotta
¼ cup artichoke crowns, finely chopped
1 tbs. tomatoes, peeled, seeded, chopped
1 green onion, minced
1 tbs. Parmesan cheese
1 tbs. Worcestershire sauce
salt and freshly ground pepper

Combine all ingredients, mix well and refrigerate for 2-3 hours before serving. This keeps well in the refrigerator for 2-3 days.

Nutritional information per ¼ cup 60 calories, 3 grams fat, 2 grams saturated fat, 1 gram polyunsaturated fat, 1 gram monounsaturated fat, 4 grams protein, 4 grams carbohydrate, 8 mg cholesterol, 137+ mg sodium

Cucumber Dip

½ cup

This is a refreshing Middle Eastern-flavored dip. It is great with crisp pita chips or fresh vegetables. Or put a spoonful or two in a pita pocket with grilled flank steak or chicken.

¼ cup cucumber, finely grated
¼ cup lowfat yogurt
¼ cup light sour cream
¼ tsp. cumin
1 tbs. fresh cilantro, minced
¼ tsp. hot chili pepper, chopped (optional)
dash cayenne
salt and freshly ground pepper

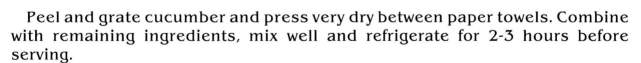

Peel and grate cucumber and press very dry between paper towels. Combine with remaining ingredients, mix well and refrigerate for 2-3 hours before serving.

Nutritional information per ¼ cup 62 calories, 4 grams fat, 3 grams saturated fat, 0 grams polyunsaturated fat, 1 gram monounsaturated fat, 3 grams protein, 4 grams carbohydrate, 14 mg cholesterol, 33+ mg sodium

Teriyaki Beef Rollups

Very thinly sliced beef is dipped into teriyaki sauce, rolled around crisp vegetable sticks and broiled for a delicious snack or the lunch box. These keep well in the refrigerator, so make several.

2 tbs. teriyaki sauce
¼ tsp. brown sugar
¼ tsp. fresh ginger, grated
2 (1 oz. each) slices beef,
    thinly sliced

2 strips red **or** green pepper, ¼" x 4"
2 green beans **or** 2 strips carrot ¼" x 4",
    cooked crisp tender

Preheat broiler. Combine teriyaki sauce, brown sugar and grated ginger on a plate. Dip beef slices in sauce and marinate 5-10 minutes. Remove; place one strip of red or green pepper and one green bean or carrot strip on each piece of meat. Use red with green or orange with green for an attractive color combination. Roll up, place on broiler rack and broil 3-4 minutes each side, turning once. To serve, trim both ends and slice each roll into 3-4 pieces, cutting on the diagonal so the colors of the vegetables show. To make 10 rolls, use ½ cup teriyaki sauce, 1 tsp. brown sugar and 1 tsp. grated ginger.

Nutritional information per roll 75 calories, 2 grams fat, 1 gram saturated fat, 0 grams polyunsaturated fat, 1 gram monounsaturated fat, 10 grams protein, 5 grams carbohydrate, 20 mg cholesterol, 700+ mg sodium

Sandwiches and Fillings

Sandwiches are generally the first things that come to mind when planning a lunch. A tasty filling sandwiched between two pieces of bread is very portable and easy to eat. A good, honest loaf of bread with a fragrant yeasty taste really makes the sandwich and is worth a search. Buy a different kind of bread at the deli or the bakery once or twice a month to expand your sandwich menus. In addition to bread, think about rolls: hard, soft, whole wheat, rye, onion rolls; bagels, croissants, or mini pita breads. And don't limit sandwich fillings to bread. Consider spreading large crisp crackers, Ryecrisp, Cracklebred, Kavli Thins, Finn Crisp or Wasa Breads with a creamy filling just before you eat.

Light cream cheese incorporating mustard or horseradish, crisp vegetable bits or pickles makes a wonderful sandwich spread or a base for some sliced meats. Crisp lettuce leaves, sprouts, sliced pickles or onions, tomatoes, roasted or fresh red or green pepper strips, marinated cucumbers all add to the flavor, texture and moistness to a sandwich. Carry the lettuce, tomato and cucumber slices separately and add just before eating. Place pickles, pepper strips and other moist additions in the middle of the sandwich between slices of meat or cheese to keep them from soaking into the bread. Consider using olive oil and a sprinkle of vinegar on a roll or bread slice instead of mayonnaise and mustard. Or moisten canned corned beef with a little buttermilk. Keep two or three different kinds of mustard in the refrigerator to add a little spice to your sandwich.

Be Creative with Sandwich Combinations (page 103) ▶

Be Creative with Sandwich Combinations

Here are a few different sandwich combinations to consider for a delicious lunch.

- Smoked turkey slices, thin apple slices dipped in lemon juice and light cream cheese mixed with a blue veined cheese.
- Thin roasted pork slices with mayonnaise, horseradish and sliced pickled beets on light rye.
- Smoked sliced salmon, capers or cucumbers and light cream cheese on rye.
- Salad shrimp, diced celery, chopped parsley and a generous dash of cayenne with mayonnaise on a croissant.
- Chopped egg and green stuffed olives with mayonnaise and lettuce in a pita bread or croissant.
- Light cream cheese with chopped peanuts, chutney, roast chicken slices and a crisp lettuce leaf on whole wheat bread.
- Cut the end off a small soft roll, scoop out most of the inside and fill with eggs scrambled with sliced green onions or fresh chopped tomato pieces. Eat at room temperature or reheat in a microwave.

◀ Arams (page 104)

- Combine cubes of roast pork or turkey, diced green chilies, chopped cilantro with mustard and light cream cheese. Fill a sandwich roll and take some sliced tomatoes to add just before eating.
- Spread mustard on dark rye bread; top with drained canned sardines, Monterey Jack cheese and thinly sliced onion rings.
- Make a beef salad of finely chopped roast beef, sweet pickles, stone ground mustard and mayonnaise. Spread on whole wheat bread or crisp crackers.
- Put some mayonnaise inside a pita pocket and fill with slices of ripe avocado, tomato, Gouda cheese and some crunchy sprouts.
- Thinly slice some boiled beef brisket and fill a pita pocket along with lettuce leaves and a dollop of prepared Thousand Island dressing.

All about Arams - Armenian Cracker Bread Rolls

Armenian cracker bread, also known as Lavosh, is available in packages of 3-5 large 15"-16" rounds or square pieces. There are plain, sesame seed and whole wheat varieties available.

To soften the large sheets for filling and rolling, prepare a work space covered with a large damp towel. Moisten one of the large pieces on both sides with water by running it under the faucet, wetting both sides. Place the cracker bread on the damp towel, cover with another damp towel and let rest about 45 minutes to 1 hour until it is soft enough to roll. The time needed depends on the thickness of the cracker bread and how moist it is. If there are dry spots, sprinkle on a little more water. A spritz bottle works well for this.

Soft cream cheese spread over the soft cracker bread provides a good base to hold the rest of the filling ingredients. Season the cream cheese with herbs, mustard or horseradish, or use it plain. For a 15" or 16" bread use about 3-4 ozs. of softened cream cheese. Spread the cheese to the edges of the cracker bread. Top with some thinly sliced ham, roast beef, turkey, a fairly finely chopped meat salad mixture, sliced cheeses, some strips of roasted peppers, or thinly sliced onions and tomatoes or whatever combination you like. Roll up the cracker bread from the long side like a jelly roll, rolling as tightly as possible without breaking. Cover with the same damp towel, slip into a plastic bag and refrigerate for an hour before serving. Cut roll into 1"-1½" pieces to serve. This can be made a day ahead and removed from the refrigerator for an hour before serving.

Be creative!
- Spread with smoked salmon mixed with dilled cream cheese, cucumber and onion slices.
- Spread with chicken salad, black olives and sun-dried tomatoes.
- Spread with **Mediterranean Salad**, page 33.

Celery Root, Prosciutto and Cheese Aram

12 sandwiches

This filling makes a delicious salad on its own, but is particularly nice rolled in softened cracker bread.

1 large softened cracker bread (see instructions, page 104)
1 small celery root, about 8-10 ozs.
1 cup Swiss **or** smoked Gouda cheese, grated
1 tbs. Dijon mustard
1 tbs. red wine vinegar
1 tsp. lemon juice
¼ cup full-flavored olive oil
2 tbs. parsley, minced
3-4 ozs. light cream cheese, softened
12 very thin slices prosciutto

Peel celery root and grate with a medium shredding disk in the food processor. There should be about 1¾-2 cups of grated celery root. Use same shredding disk for cheese. In a medium mixing bowl combine mustard, red wine vinegar, lemon juice and olive oil. Beat with a fork or whisk until ingredients form an emulsion. Add grated celery root, cheese and parsley to dressing. Toss with 2 forks to mix well. Spread softened cracker bread with cream cheese. Top with celery root, cheese mixture and thin ham slices. Gently roll up like a jelly roll, as tightly as possible. Wrap in damp towel until ready to serve. Refrigerate for at least an hour to make cutting easier. Cut in 1"-1½" slices. This may be made a day ahead.

Nutritional information per sandwich   210 calories, 12 grams fat, 5 grams saturated fat, 2 grams polyunsaturated fat, 6 grams monounsaturated fat, 9 grams protein, 16 grams carbohydrate, 22 grams cholesterol, 165 mg sodium

Be creative!   If there is extra celery root and cheese mixture, serve it in a lettuce cup or use it for a cold jumbo shell stuffing.

Grilled Flank Steak for Pita Pockets

Servings: 6

This grilled flank steak is wonderful with a baked potato and fresh vegetable for dinner, but be sure to save some of these very thin slices for your pita pocket or hard French roll for a next day lunch box treat.

1 flank steak, about 1 lb.,
   trimmed of all fat
grated lemon peel from 1 lemon
2 tbs. fresh lemon juice
2 tbs. peanut oil

2 tbs. light soy sauce
1 tsp. fresh ginger, grated
1 clove garlic, finely minced
freshly ground black pepper

Place flank steak in a flat pan with sides. Grate lemon peel over steak. Add lemon juice, oil, soy sauce, fresh ginger, garlic and pepper to steak in pan. Turn steak over once or twice to coat both sides with lemon peel, ginger and garlic pieces. Marinate about 30 minutes. Grill 3-4 minutes a side on the barbecue, or place under a very hot broiler. Do not overcook. Steak should remain quite rare in the middle. Remove to a cutting board and slice very thinly on the diagonal across the grain. Refrigerate pieces to be used for sandwiches. Stuff in pita pockets or hard rolls just before eating.

Nutritional information per serving of meat only 190 calories, 10 grams fat, 3 grams saturated fat, 2 grams polyunsaturated fat, 5 grams monounsaturated fat, 22 grams protein, 1 gram carbohydrate, 60 mg cholesterol, 155+ mg sodium

Ham and Red Pepper Aram

This is a simple, basic recipe for a rolled cracker bread sandwich. Some strips of romaine lettuce without the center vein can be used to add a little crunch if you are going to serve it within an hour or two.

1 large softened cracker bread (see instructions, page 104)
3-4 ozs. light cream cheese, softened
2 red peppers, roasted, cut into strips
5 thin Danish ham slices

Beat cream cheese in a small bowl so it spreads easily. Add a little milk if necessary. Spread cream cheese evenly on cracker bread and top with red pepper strips. Add ham slices, spreading them out to the edges in 1 or 2 rows so that each slice will have both the red peppers and ham. Roll up the long way like a jelly roll, making a fairly tight roll. Wrap completely in damp towel until you are ready to serve. Refrigerate for about an hour for easier cutting. Trim ends and cut into 12 equal slices.

Nutritional information per sandwich 130 calories, 5 grams fat, 2 grams saturated fat, 1 gram polyunsaturated fat, 1 gram monounsaturated fat, 6 grams protein, 15 grams carbohydrate, 12 grams cholesterol, 160 mg sodium

All about the Pan-Bagnat

Countries ringing the Mediterranean make a wonderful stuffed roll or sandwich called pan-bagnat, which translates to "bathed bread." The roll or loaf of bread is cut almost in half, leaving one side hinged, and some of the inside is scooped out. The inside bread halves are generously moistened with olive oil, painted with anchovy paste and filled with black olives, garlic, onions, celery, tomatoes, crumbled cheese, or other good things. A little vinegar is sprinkled over the contents, the top of the roll pressed down, and it is tightly wrapped and left for a couple of hours to mellow before it is eaten. Pan-bagnats can be made of small rolls as well as round or long loaves, depending on number of people to be served. If filled with sliced meats and cheeses, grill it over the fire, or put it under the broiler for a few minutes to crisp the outside and melt the cheese. Heating is not necessary and it is delicious at room temperature.

There are infinite combinations of ingredients to be used, so put together your favorite flavors.

Pan-Bagnat

Here is a traditional type filling for a small hard roll.

Dressing:

1 tbs. **Garlic-Flavored Olive Oil**, page 48

1 tsp. red wine vinegar

¼ tsp. Dijon mustard

freshly ground pepper

For each sandwich:

1 sandwich roll

prepared olive paste

crumbled feta cheese

pimiento strips

capers

fresh tomato pieces

2 marinated artichoke crowns,
   slivered

Cut roll in half, leaving one side hinged, and scoop out most of the soft insides. Drizzle dressing generously on both halves. Spread olive paste on both halves and fill with crumbled feta cheese, pimiento, capers, tomato pieces and artichoke pieces. Drizzle a little more dressing over filling and close roll, pressing halves firmly together. Wrap tightly and let mellow for 2 hours before eating. Refrigerate if sandwich is not going to be consumed in a few hours.

Nutritional information per serving 335 calories, 20 grams fat, 4 grams saturated fat, 3 grams polyunsaturated fat, 11 grams monounsaturated fat, 7 grams protein, 34 grams carbohydrate, 7 mg cholesterol, 580+ mg sodium.

Meat and Cheese Pan-Bagnat

Servings: 1

This is a heartier version of a stuffed roll.

Dressing:

1 tbs. **Garlic-Flavored Olive Oil**, page 48

1 tsp. red wine vinegar

¼ tsp. Dijon mustard

freshly ground pepper

For each serving:

1 sandwich roll

1 oz. grated Swiss **or**
   cheddar cheese

2 thin slices cooked turkey

2 thin slices pastrami

capers

chopped pimiento

fresh tomato pieces

thinly sliced red onion rings

Cut sandwich roll in half, pull out most of soft insides and paint both sides generously with dressing. Fill with cheese, meats, capers, pimiento, tomato pieces and onion rings. Sprinkle filling with more dressing and close roll, pressing halves firmly together. Wrap tightly and let flavors develop for 1-2 hours in refrigerator before eating.

Nutritional information per serving   650 calories, 34 grams fat, 11 grams saturated fat, 4 grams polyunsaturated fat, 16 grams monounsaturated fat, 38 grams protein, 60 grams carbohydrate, 84 mg cholesterol, 1400 mg sodium

Vegetable Sandwich Spread

½ cup

This spread can be made with your choice of chopped vegetables. Part of its charm is the color variation.

4 ozs. light cream cheese
2 radishes, chopped
2 tbs. celery, chopped
2 tbs. carrot, grated
2 tbs. red **or** green pepper, chopped
1 small green onion, thinly sliced
3-4 drops Tabasco
salt and freshly ground pepper
chopped parsley for garnish

Combine all ingredients except parsley in a small bowl. Refrigerate until ready to use.

Nutritional information per 2 tbs. 102 calories, 10 grams fat, 6 grams saturated fat, 0 grams polyunsaturated fat, 3 grams monounsaturated fat, 2 grams protein, 1 gram carbohydrate, 31 mg cholesterol, 89+ mg sodium

---

Be creative!

- Spread on Wasa Crispbread or Cracklebred, top with another piece and dip edges of filled crispbread in chopped parsley.
- Use spread to stuff celery or fennel pieces, or fill cherry tomatoes.
- Stuff mushrooms: twist off stems of medium mushrooms, scoop out a little indentation where the stem was, dip whole mushrooms in lemon juice and fill with spread.
- Start with light cream cheese: add chopped green chilies, fresh red peppers, chopped cilantro and a dash of cumin.
- Or try light cream cheese, smoked salmon, capers, dill and chopped celery.
- Or light cream cheese, chopped sun-dried tomato pieces, black olives, fresh parsley and fresh thyme.

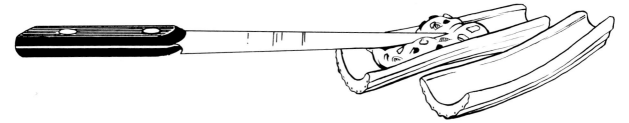

Handpies

Many cuisines include a portable sandwich wrapped in a baked, fried or steamed dough. The Russians have their piroshki, the Mexicans their empanadas, and the English their pasties and pork pies. Handpies can be very substantial, especially those enclosed in a short crust with a rich meat filling. Once you have mastered the basic techniques, the creative variations are endless. We have included recipes using basic bread dough, a short crust and packaged puff pastry dough. Fillings range from light to heavy enough for a growing boy or hard-working man. Feel free to mix and match fillings and crusts.

Baked or steamed handpies can be individually wrapped and frozen. Remove from freezer in the morning and they will be perfect by lunchtime. If desired wrap in a paper towel and warm in a microwave.

Basic Yeast Dough Wrapper

10 pieces

Frozen bread dough makes an easy and delicious handpie wrapper. Remove a 1 lb. loaf from freezer and allow to thaw at room temperature for about 45 minutes until it is soft enough to divide into the desired number of pieces. Cut with a knife, lightly flour the pieces and cover loosely with plastic wrap. Allow to rise until double in size and proceed with the recipe.

Puff Pastry Shell Crust

Remove frozen pattie shells from the freezer, uncover and allow to defrost at room temperature for 20 minutes. Lightly flour and roll out to a 6" circle. With top side up, prick all over with tines of a fork. Place 2-3 tablespoons of filling on one half of the pastry, leaving a ½" border. Brush edges with water, fold over the top half of the dough and seal well by pressing down with tines of a fork. Bake in a preheated 425° oven about 25 minutes until puffed and nicely browned.

Rich Handpie Crust

*This basic crust can be used with **Cornish Pasties**, page 132, **Jamaican Patties**, page 128, and **South-of-the-Border Empanadas**, page 132.*

2 cups all purpose flour
¼ tsp. baking powder
½ tsp. salt
1 egg yolk
½ cup vegetable shortening
about ⅓ cup ice water

Add flour, baking powder and salt to bowl of food processor. Pulse once or twice to combine. Add egg yolk and shortening and pulse until mixture resembles coarse meal. With processor running, slowly add ice water until mixture comes together. Remove from bowl, wrap in plastic wrap and refrigerate for ½ hour or longer before rolling out.

Tuna and Rice Piroshki

Russian in feeling, these small filled buns are easily made from a 1 lb. loaf of frozen bread dough.

1 (1 lb.) loaf frozen bread dough
1 (6½ ozs.) can water pack tuna
⅔ cup cooked rice
3 tbs. light sour cream

2 tbs. canned diced green chilies
1 hard-boiled egg, chopped
salt and freshly ground pepper
1 egg for egg wash

Defrost dough and divide into 10 equal sized pieces. When pieces have risen to double in size, dust lightly with flour and flatten into disks about 2" in diameter. Cover again with plastic wrap, and allow dough to relax while preparing the filling. Drain tuna well and place in a medium sized mixing bowl. Stir with a fork to break up into smaller pieces. Add remaining ingredients and mix well. Assemble and bake as for **Meat Piroshki**, page 122.

Nutritional information per piroshki   215 calories, 1 gram fat, 1 gram saturated fat, 0 grams polyunsaturated fat, 1 gram monounsaturated fat, 12 grams protein, 33 grams carbohydrate, 40 mg cholesterol, 410+ mg sodium

Meat Piroshki

This Russian classic is often deep-fried and eaten hot with soup. They are equally good when baked.

1 (1 lb.) loaf frozen bread dough
1 tbs. vegetable oil
1 medium yellow onion, chopped
½ lb. lean ground beef
¼ cup light sour cream
2 tsp. fresh **or** ½ tsp. dried dill
2 tsp. Worcestershire sauce
salt and freshly ground pepper
1 egg for egg wash

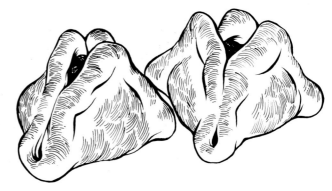

Defrost dough and divide into 10 equal sized pieces. When pieces have risen to double in size, dust lightly with flour and flatten into disks about 2" in diameter. Cover again with plastic wrap and allow dough to relax while preparing filling. Heat oil in a frying pan over medium heat and add onion. When onion is translucent, but not brown, add ground beef and break up with a spatula. Sauté until beef is cooked through and lightly browned. Remove from heat and allow to cool. Stir in sour cream and dill. Preheat oven to 375°. To assemble, take a disk of dough and roll with a rolling pin until it is about 3½" in diameter. Put about 2 tbs. filling in center of disk and fold up sides around filling. Pinch dough to seal and place sealed side up on an oiled baking sheet. Assemble remaining piroshki. Cover again with plastic wrap and allow to raise in a warm, draft-free place for about 30 minutes. Brush with egg wash (one egg and 2 tsp. water, beaten with a fork until well combined). Bake in a preheated 375° oven for 15-20 minutes until golden brown. Cool on a rack. Can be eaten either hot or at room temperature. Reheat in a microwave before serving if desired.

Nutritional information per piroshki 255 calories, 9 grams fat, 4 grams saturated fat, 1 gram polyunsaturated fat, 4 grams monounsaturated fat, 13 grams protein, 31 grams carbohydrate, 54 mg cholesterol, 360+ mg sodium

Be Creative! Bring up sides in a "three cornered hat" shape and pinch together sides, leaving ½" opening at top.

Chinese Steamed Buns

The classic Chinese dim sum, these tasty buns can be enjoyed anytime.

1 cup all purpose flour
1 cup cake flour
2 tbs. sugar
2½ tsp. baking powder
⅔ cup milk
1 tbs. vegetable shortening
1 cup Chinese style barbecued pork, diced
2 tsp. peanut oil

1 tbs. tomato catsup
1 tbs. oyster sauce
2 tsp. soy sauce
1 tsp. sugar
1½ tsp. cornstarch
finely ground white pepper
¼ cup water
¼ tsp. sesame oil

Add flour, sugar and baking powder to the bowl of food processor. Pulse to mix well. Add shortening and pulse again to combine. With processor running, add milk and process until dough forms a ball. Turn out dough onto a lightly floured board and knead for 1-2 minutes. Dough will be quite soft. Form dough into a log about 12" long. Cover loosely with plastic wrap and allow to rest while preparing filling. In a small bowl mix catsup, oyster sauce, soy sauce, sugar, cornstarch, pepper and water. Stir well to blend. Add peanut oil to a small nonstick frying pan over medium heat. Add diced meat, stir to warm and coat with oil. Add sauce mixture, reduce heat and simmer until sauce thickens, stirring frequently. Remove from heat, stir in sesame oil and allow to cool. Cut dough into 8 equal sized pieces. To form buns, take a piece of dough and create a depression in the middle with your thumb. Put about 2 tbs. of filling in the depression and pull up sides of dough. Pleat and pinch dough to seal top. Place each bun on a 2" square of parchment or waxed paper. Steam over rapidly boiling water for 10 minutes. These buns freeze well. Serve at room temperature or reheat by steaming over hot water for a few minutes or heat briefly in a microwave.

Nutritional information per bun   220 calories, 6 grams fat, 2 grams saturated fat, 1 gram polyunsaturated fat, 3 grams monounsaturated fat, 10 grams protein, 30 grams carbohydrate, 18 mg cholesterol, 335 mg sodium

Calzone

The choice of good things to put into a calzone, first cousin to a pizza, is almost endless. Start with this traditional combination of fillings, and then take off on your own. Make smaller ones by dividing dough into 6 pieces.

1 (1 lb.) loaf frozen bread dough
4 oz. mozzarella cheese, shredded
4 oz. ham **or** salami **or** mortadella, cut into thin strips
1 (4 ozs.) can mushroom stems and pieces, drained
1 small onion, thinly sliced
3 tbs. Parmesan cheese, grated
½ tsp. dried oregano
½ tsp. basil
freshly ground pepper **or** a few red pepper flakes

Defrost frozen bread dough. When it is soft enough to cut, divide into 4 equal sized pieces. Lightly flour dough pieces, cover loosely with plastic wrap and allow to rise until double in size. Roll each piece of dough into a circle about 8" in diameter. Put mozzarella cheese on one half of dough, leaving a ¾" border.

Top with meat strips, mushrooms and onion slices. Sprinkle on Parmesan cheese, oregano, basil and pepper. Fold top half of dough over to make a half moon and pinch dough together to seal. Preheat oven to 375°. Place on a lightly oiled cookie sheet and allow dough to rise for 15 minutes. Brush lightly with olive oil and bake until nicely brown, about 25 minutes.

Nutritional information per calzone   490 calories, 18 grams fat, 9 grams saturated fat, 2 grams polyunsaturated fat, 6 grams monounsaturated fat, 23 grams protein, 60 grams carbohydrate, 46 mg cholesterol, 1200 mg sodium

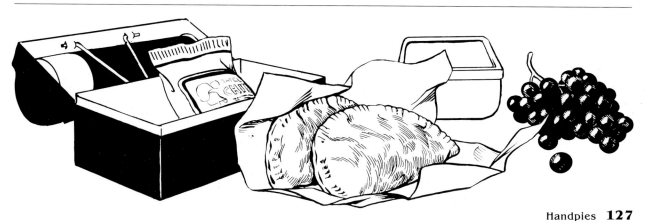

Jamaican Patties

Authentic patties are made with Scotch Bonnet peppers, and can range from spicy to searing hot. One chopped jalapeno pepper makes a spicy but not hot patty. If you enjoy hot food, add more peppers or adjust cooked filling with pepper sauce.

1 recipe **Rich Handpie Crust**, page 118 , with ½ tsp.
   curry powder added to the dry ingredients
1 tbs. vegetable oil
1 jalapeno pepper, stem and seeds removed, minced
2 tsp. curry powder
½ lb. lean ground beef
4 slices fresh white bread, crust removed, cut into small cubes
⅓ cup milk
salt and freshly ground pepper
hot pepper sauce (optional)

Add oil to nonstick frying pan over medium heat. Add pepper, onions and curry powder and sauté for 1-2 minutes. Add beef and stir to crumble. Cook over medium heat until beef is cooked but not brown. Soak bread cubes in milk until thoroughly moistened. Add soaked cubes, milk, salt and pepper to meat and simmer until mixture will hold its shape, but is still moist. Allow to cool. Roll out pastry to a thickness of ⅛", and using a small saucer as a guide, cut rounds about 4" in diameter. Place 2-3 tbs. filling on one half of the dough. Fold over other half of dough and seal edges by crimping with a fork. Prick top in several places to allow steam to escape. Preheat oven to 375°. Place patties on a cookie sheet; bake 15-20 minutes until oven golden brown. Cool on a rack. Eat at room temperature or reheat in a conventional or microwave oven.

Nutritional information per patty 465 calories, 26 grams fat, 8 grams saturated fat, 5 grams polyunsaturated fat, 11 grams monounsaturated fat, 16 grams protein, 40 grams carbohydrate, 70 mg cholesterol, 300+ mg sodium

South-of-the-Border Empanadas

You can make these full sized for a substantial meal, or in miniature for an appetizer or to go with a salad or soup.

1 recipe of **Rich Handpie Crust**, page 118
2 tbs. raisins
1 tbs. vegetable oil
½ lb. lean ground pork **or** ground beef
1 tomato, peeled, seeded, chopped **or** ⅔ cup canned
    tomatoes with some of their juice
1 small onion, chopped
2 tbs. toasted slivered almonds **or** toasted pine nuts
⅛ tsp. cinnamon
1 tsp. cider vinegar
salt and freshly ground pepper

Put raisins in a small bowl and cover with warm water to soften. Add vegetable oil and onion to a nonstick frying pan over medium heat. Sauté onion until translucent. Add meat in a thin layer and stir to break up. Continue cooking until meat is lightly brown. Drain excess fat from pan and add tomato. Continue to cook until sauce thickens and mixture is quite dry. Remove from heat and stir in drained raisins, nuts, cinnamon, vinegar, salt and pepper. Preheat oven to 375°. Divide handpie pastry into 6 equal sized pieces and roll each piece of dough to a circle about 4" in diameter. Place 2-3 tbs. filling on one half of the dough. Fold over the other half and seal by crimping with a fork. Place on a baking sheet and prick top in several places to allow steam to escape. Bake until golden brown, about 20 minutes. Cool on a rack.

Nutritional information per empanada   435 calories, 28 grams fat, 7 grams saturated fat, 7 grams polyunsaturated fat, 12 grams monounsaturated fat, 9 grams protein, 37 grams carbohydrate, 50 mg cholesterol, 445+ mg sodium

Cornish Pasties

6 pasties

The British are very fond of all kinds of pies. This is a version of the traditional lunch of Cornish miners.

1 recipe **Rich Handpie Crust** , page 118
1 small boiling potato, diced (about ⅔ cup)
1 small carrot, diced (about ⅔ cup)
½ lb. lean ground beef
¼ cup onion, finely chopped
1 tbs. parsley, minced
1 small clove garlic, minced (optional)
salt and freshly ground pepper
1 egg yolk
2 tsp. milk

Cut carrot and potato into ⅜" dice. Boil in salted water until just tender, 7-10 minutes. Drain well in a sieve. In a bowl mix beef, onion, parsley and garlic. Add potato and carrot and gently incorporate into meat mixture with your hands. Preheat oven to 350°. Divide pastry into 6 equal sized pieces, and roll each piece into a circle about ⅛" thick. Place ⅙ of the meat mixture on ½ of the circle, leaving a border around the edge. Fold top half of dough over to make a half moon and seal edges by pressing down with tines of a fork. Place on a lightly oiled cookie sheet. Brush with egg wash (1 egg yolk and 2 tsp milk, beaten together). Cut a small slit in the top of each pasty to allow steam to escape. Bake for 45 minutes. Allow to cool on a rack. May be eaten at room temperature or reheated in a microwave.

Nutritional information per pasty 445 calories, 26 grams fat, 7 grams saturated fat, 5 grams polyunsaturated fat, 11 grams monounsaturated fat, 15 grams protein, 38 grams carbohydrate, 68 mg cholesterol, 235+ mg sodium

Be Creative! Bake standing on the folded side to resemble cocks' combs.

Sloppy Joe Buns

These freeze well and reheat in the microwave. Make a batch on the weekend and pull from the freezer in the morning.

1 (1 lb.) loaf frozen bread dough
1 lb. lean ground beef
1 (15½ ozs.) can Manwich Sloppy Joe Mix
1 egg for egg wash

Defrost frozen bread dough until it is soft enough to cut into 10 equal sized pieces. Brown ground beef in a skillet. Drain fat. Add Manwich sauce, stir and simmer for 5 minutes, or until sauce is very thick. Cool and fill bread dough as for **Meat Piroshki**, page 122. Preheat oven to 375°. Cover assembled buns loosely with plastic wrap, and let rise for 30 minutes. Brush with egg wash and bake for 15-20 minutes until golden brown. Reheat in a microwave before serving.

Nutritional information per bun 150 calories, 9 grams fat, 3 grams saturated fat, 0 grams polyunsaturated fat, 4 grams monounsaturated fat, 12 grams protein, 6 grams carbohydrate, 40 mg cholesterol, 330 mg sodium

Hearty Lunches

Substantial lunches are required for people doing rigorous physical work, for athletes and for growing boys. Consider packing an extra sandwich and adding a wedge of cheese or a can of sardines and crackers. Pack crisp vegetable sticks and bread sticks or pita chips with dip, or stuff celery or fennel with a cheese spread. Tortilla chips and prepared salsa would also round out the lunch box. Don't forget a piece of fruit, a pudding cup, or some cookies.

Baked **Stuffed Potato**, **Meatball Stew Sandwich**, and **Macaroni Lunch Box Special** are all suitable when more calories are required. Or try the baked egg dishes we've included.

Mexican Style Stuffed Potato

Servings: 1

This potato is stuffed with canned green chilies and salsa. Make it as spicy as you like.

1 (8 ozs.) baking potato
3 tbs. light sour cream
2 tbs. hot **or** mild prepared salsa
¼ cup canned green chilies, diced

salt and freshly ground pepper
¼ tsp. cumin
1 oz. Monterey Jack cheese,
   coarsely grated

Preheat oven to 450°. Lightly oil potato skin, place on oven rack and bake until done. Cut baked potato in half. When cool enough to handle, scrape out pulp from each half and place in a medium bowl. Add sour cream, salsa, green chilies, cumin, salt, pepper and ½ of the grated cheese to potato mixture. Combine and stuff back into two shells. Top with remaining grated cheese. Reheat in a microwave just before serving. Or heat, wrap in foil, and pack in insulated container to keep warm.

Nutritional information per serving 460 calories, 18 grams fat, 13 grams saturated fat, 1 gram polyunsaturated fat, 3 grams monounsaturated fat, 14 grams protein, 64 grams carbohydrate, 26 mg cholesterol, 250+ mg sodium

---

Macaroni Lunch Box Special (page 144) ▶

Greek Style Stuffed Potato

Servings: 1

Potatoes can be combined with so many different ingredients for new taste treats. A few black olives and some feta cheese make these potatoes different and delicious.

1 (8 ozs.) baking potato	½ tsp. capers
2 tbs. light sour cream	1 tbs. pimiento, diced
1 oz. feta cheese, diced	salt and freshly ground pepper
4-5 black olives, pitted, chopped	grated Parmesan cheese

Preheat oven to 450°. Lightly oil potato skin with vegetable oil, place on oven rack and bake until done. Cut baked potato in half. When cool enough to handle, scoop out pulp into a small bowl. Add sour cream, feta cheese, olives, capers, pimiento pieces, salt and pepper to taste. Mix well and stuff potato shells with mixture. Top with Parmesan cheese. Reheat in a microwave or heat and pack in insulated bag to keep warm.

Nutritional information per serving   430 calories, 17 grams fat, 11 grams saturated fat, 1 gram polyunsaturated fat, 5 grams monounsaturated fat, 12 grams protein, 62 grams carbohydrate, 28 mg cholesterol, 560+ mg sodium

---

◀ **Fresh Fruit with Orange Yogurt Sauce (page 157)**

Stuffed Potato

This potato is very satisfying. Low in fat, high in fiber and nutrition, and plenty of calories if you need them. And if you don't, just take half a potato for a healthy light lunch. It reheats beautifully in a microwave.

1 (8 ozs.) baking potato
1 tbs. onion, finely minced
1 tsp. olive oil
⅓ cup plain lowfat yogurt
1 tsp. Dijon mustard

1 tbs. Parmesan cheese
1 tbs. fresh tomato **or** roasted
   red pepper, chopped
1 tbs. sharp cheddar cheese, grated
salt and freshly ground pepper

Preheat oven to 450°. Lightly oil potato skin, place on oven rack and bake until done. Sauté onion in olive oil until translucent. Set aside to cool. When cool, add remaining ingredients except cheddar cheese. When potato is done, cut in half. Scrape out mixture from each half and place in a medium bowl. Add sauce mixture and mix well; stuff back into potato shells. Top with grated cheddar. Before serving, reheat in a microwave until steaming hot and the cheese melts.

Nutritional information per serving 420 calories, 9 grams fat, 3 grams saturated fat, 1 gram polyunsaturated fat, 5 grams monounsaturated fat, 14 grams protein, 72 grams carbohydrate, 12 mg cholesterol, 280+ mg sodium

Be creative!

- Add diced ham.
- Add chopped olives.
- Add sliced green onions.
- Add shelled roasted sunflower seeds.
- Add chopped cilantro.

Spinach and Mushroom Stuffed Potato

Servings: 1

If you plan to have leftover cooked spinach, this goes together very quickly.

1 (8 ozs.) baking potato
1 tbs. olive oil
2 tbs. shallots **or** green onions, minced
1 small clove garlic, minced
¼ cup mushrooms, thinly sliced
¼ cup spinach, cooked, finely chopped

salt and freshly ground pepper
2 tbs. ricotta cheese
1 tbs. Dijon mustard
1 tsp. parsley, minced
1 oz. Swiss cheese,
    coarsely shredded

Preheat oven to 450°. Lightly oil potato skin with vegetable oil. Place on oven rack and bake until done. In a small skillet, heat oil and sauté shallots, garlic and mushrooms for 3-4 minutes until soft. Add cooked spinach, salt and pepper. Cook for another minute. When potato is cool enough to handle, cut it in half and scoop out pulp. Place pulp in a small bowl with shallots and mushroom mixture. Add ricotta, mustard and parsley and mix well. Stuff potato halves with mixture and top with shredded Swiss cheese. Reheat in a microwave before serving, or heat, wrap well and place in an insulated container to keep warm.

Nutritional information per serving 550 calories, 25 grams fat, 8 grams saturated fat, 2 grams polyunsaturated fat, 13 grams monounsaturated fat, 20 grams protein, 66 grams carbohydrate, 36 mg cholesterol, 360+ mg sodium

Stuffed Sweet Potato

Sweet potatoes make a good, nutritious variation on the stuffed potato theme. They would be good just with a little butter and orange juice.

1 (8 ozs.) sweet potato
1 tbs. brown sugar
1 tbs. light sour cream

2 tbs. pecans, chopped
salt and freshly ground pepper
whole pecans for garnish

Preheat oven to 450°. Bake sweet potato until soft. Remove from oven; when cool enough to handle, cut in half and scoop out pulp. Combine pulp with brown sugar, sour cream, pecans, salt and pepper. Restuff potato halves. Garnish each half with 2-3 whole pecans. Reheat in a microwave.

Nutritional information per serving 375 calories, 21 grams fat, 3 grams saturated fat, 5 grams polyunsaturated fat, 13 grams monounsaturated fat, 5 grams protein, 47 grams carbohydrate, 6 mg cholesterol, 12+ mg sodium

Be creative! Combine pulp with 1 tbs. honey, 1 tbs. light sour cream and some chopped fresh pineapple pieces.

Macaroni Lunch Box Special

Macaroni, like potatoes, can be combined with many different flavors for a completely new look. Here is a mildly spicy, cheesed version to be heated and carried in a vacuum bottle, or heated in a microwave just before eating.

4 ozs. dried elbow macaroni
2 tbs. butter
2 tbs. flour
1 cup milk
1 tsp. Worcestershire sauce
½ tsp. dried mustard

¼ cup Parmesan cheese
¼ cup canned green chilies, chopped
salt and finely ground white pepper
2 (½ oz. each) slices cheddar **or**
  Monterey Jack cheese

Cook macaroni according to package directions. Melt butter in a small saucepan. Add flour and cook 2 minutes. Whisk in milk; add Worcestershire sauce, mustard and Parmesan cheese. Cook, stirring, until mixture comes to a boil and thickens. Add green chilies, salt and white pepper. Combine sauce with cooked macaroni. Place in vacuum bottle or 2 microwave dishes. Top microwave dishes with cheese slices just before heating.

Nutritional information per serving 450 calories, 20 grams fat, 12 grams saturated fat, 1 gram polyunsaturated fat, 6 grams monounsaturated fat, 16 grams protein, 51 grams carbohydrate, 55 mg cholesterol, 380 mg sodium

Be creative! Substitute ¼ cup sliced stuffed green olives **or** diced roasted red peppers for the canned green chilies.

Spinach and Mushroom Frittata

This is another hearty dish to be sliced into wedges and served either warm or at room temperature. Be sure to use a nonstick skillet with an ovenproof handle so it slides right out.

½ (10 ozs.) pkg. frozen spinach
1 tbs. olive oil
4-5 large mushrooms, sliced
5 green onions, thinly sliced
1 clove garlic, minced
4 eggs

1 tbs. Dijon mustard
salt and freshly ground pepper
1 tsp. dried sweet basil
dash nutmeg
3 tbs. Parmesan cheese, grated
1 tbs. light olive oil

Preheat oven to 325°. Cook spinach according to package directions. Drain and squeeze as dry as possible. If using fresh cooked spinach, use about ½ cup firmly packed chopped cooked spinach. In a 7"-8" nonstick skillet with ovenproof handle, heat olive oil and sauté mushrooms, green onions and garlic until mushrooms are cooked. Set aside. In a medium bowl combine eggs, mustard, salt and pepper, sweet basil, nutmeg and 2 tbs. Parmesan cheese. Add cooked mushroom mixture. Wipe out skillet, heat remaining 1 tbs.

oil, and pour in egg and spinach mixture. Cook over very low heat until eggs set on the bottom. Sprinkle with remaining tablespoon of Parmesan cheese and place in oven. Bake for 5-10 minutes until top is set and frittata is lightly browned. Slip out onto a plate lined with paper towels and blot off any excess oil. Transfer to another dish. Cut into 4 wedges. Serve warm or at room temperature.

Nutritional information per wedge 170 calories, 13 grams fat, 3 grams saturated fat, 1 gram polyunsaturated fat, 7 grams monounsaturated fat, 9 grams protein, 4 grams carbohydrate, 210 mg cholesterol, 170+ mg sodium

Meatball Stew Sandwich

Take the stew in a vacuum bottle or reheat in the microwave. Fill the toasted rolls just before serving, and eat with a knife and fork. This hearty, satisfying dish will be a sure hit with growing kids and ``meat and potato'' men.

1 tbs. vegetable oil
¼ cup onion, minced
½ lb. lean ground beef
¼ cup cracker crumbs
1 egg
2 tbs. parsley, minced
salt and freshly ground pepper
1 (4 ozs.) can sliced mushrooms, drained
4 ozs. cooked potato, cut into ½" cubes
1 (10½ ozs.) can beef gravy
2 ozs. dry sherry **or** red wine
4 hollowed-out toasted dinner rolls

Place vegetable oil in a small frying pan over medium heat and sauté onion until it is soft but not brown. Remove from heat. In a mixing bowl add ground beef, cracker crumbs, egg, parsley, salt and pepper. Remove onion from frying pan, leaving oil, and add to ground beef mixture. Mix well with hands and form into ½" meatballs. When all meatballs are formed, place frying pan back on heat. When hot add meatballs and brown on all sides. Remove meatballs from pan with a slotted spoon. Pour off fat from pan. Add beef gravy and wine to pan and bring to a boil. Return meatballs to pan and simmer gently for 10 minutes. Add mushrooms and potatoes and simmer a few minutes longer. Refrigerate until needed. Reheat in microwave.

For toasted dinner rolls: buy round crusty dinner rolls about 3"-3½" in diameter. Cut off top quarter of roll just above widest part and hollow out rolls using a sharp knife. Leave about ⅜" walls all around. Paint inside of rolls with light olive oil and bake in a preheated 350° oven for 10-15 minutes, until lightly brown.

Nutritional information per serving   500 calories, 25 grams fat, 7 grams saturated fat, 3 grams polyunsaturated fat, 11 grams monounsaturated fat, 25 grams protein, 46 grams carbohydrate, 105 mg cholesterol, 600+ mg sodium

---

Lunch Box Desserts

A sweet treat is a special way of rounding out the lunch box. The best and ripest fruit in season is a natural and nutritious dessert. There is a wonderful variety available, so in addition to apples or bananas, tuck in some ice cold red or green seedless grapes, a seasonal pear such as Bosc, Bartlett, Comice, or a tiny Seckel pear. During the spring and summer try fresh strawberries, a handful of deep red cherries, fresh peaches, plums, nectarines, or a couple of fresh figs with a little light cream cheese and some wholemeal biscuits or graham crackers. Or eat a good crisp apple or pear with a slice of cheddar or some blue veined cheese and walnut halves. Peel and slice a kiwi fruit and pair it with sliced oranges or melon pieces in an airtight container.

Dried fruits make a nice change of pace, and can be eaten out of hand, or cook two or three different kinds together for a compote. There are small canned fruit cups to chill, or you can make your own using a combination of fresh and frozen fruits. Baked apples can be done in minutes in a microwave and are very easy to pack. Core apples or pears, brush inside with lemon juice and fill with light cream cheese mixed with a blue veined cheese and walnuts.

Homemade snack cakes, muffins or cookies also satisfy the sweet tooth. Make ahead, wrap individually, and keep in the freezer to be pulled out at the last minute. These also help keep the other lunch items cool. Consider the animal-shaped graham crackers or cookies for the child's lunch box.

Lightly moisten a couple of paper towels and put them in a plastic sandwich bag for freshening up after some juicy fruit.

Oat Bran Apple Squares

Grated apple, nuts and cinnamon make a moist portable dessert cake for the lunch box.

3 tbs. peanut oil
¾ cup sugar
1 tsp. vanilla
2 eggs
1 cup all purpose flour
1 tsp. cinnamon
1 medium apple, peeled, coarsely grated

⅓ cup oat bran, plain **or**
   with apples and cinnamon
1 tsp. baking soda
¼ tsp. salt
¼ cup milk
½ cup pecans **or** walnuts, chopped

Preheat oven to 375°. Combine oil, sugar, vanilla and eggs in mixer bowl. Beat until well combined. Add flour, grated apple, oat bran, baking soda and milk. Mix well and stir in chopped nuts. Pour into a greased square baking pan 9" x 9" x 2" and bake for 30-35 minutes, until top springs back and toothpick comes out clean.

Nutritional information per square 130 calories, 6 grams fat, 1 gram saturated fat, 2 grams polyunsaturated fat, 2 grams monounsaturated fat, 3 grams protein, 19 grams carbohydrate, 22 mg cholesterol, 63 mg sodium

Quick Baked Apples

Oven baked apples are great, but you can have a baked apple in less than 5 minutes preparation and cooking time in a microwave, and it turns out very moist and delicious. The McIntosh variety is particularly good in this preparation.

1 baking apple, about 7 ozs.
1 tsp. brown sugar
1 tsp. white **or** dark raisins

1 tsp. pecans **or** walnuts, chopped
dash of cinnamon
1 tsp. maple syrup **or** pancake syrup

Core apple, leaving bottom stem in place. Peel approximately 1" down from the top, and using the knife blade make a cut in the skin around the apple approximately ½" down so the skin doesn't burst. Combine brown sugar, raisins, nuts and cinnamon in a small bowl. Fill apple center with mixture and top with pancake syrup. Cover tightly and microwave for 2 minutes; let stand another 2-3 minutes. This is good warm or cold, plain or with a dollop of ice cream or whipped cream.

Nutritional information per apple   200 calories, 2 grams fat, 0 grams saturated fat, 1 gram polyunsaturated fat, 1 gram monounsaturated fat, 1 gram protein, 47 grams carbohydrate, 0 mg cholesterol, 7 mg sodium

Fresh Fruit with Honey Lime Sauce

Servings: 2

This simple sauce is wonderful with cantaloupe, honeydew, casaba and Persian melons. Add a couple of strawberries, pitted bing cherries or a few blueberries for a lovely color and taste contrast.

2 cups of melon chunks
1 tbs. lime juice
½ tsp. grated lime peel
1 tbs. honey
colorful fruit for garnish

Combine grated lime juice, lime peel and honey in a small bowl and pour over fruit. Refrigerate until ready to serve.

Nutritional information per serving 100 calories, 0 grams fat, 0 grams saturated fat, 0 grams polyunsaturated fat, 0 grams monounsaturated fat, 1 gram protein, 27 grams carbohydrate, 0 mg cholesterol, 20 mg sodium

Be creative! Try on fresh papaya or peach slices.

Orange Yogurt Sauce

Just a little vanilla lowfat yogurt, honey and orange juice make a lovely creamy sauce for fresh fruit.

1 tbs. vanilla lowfat yogurt
1 tbs. orange juice
1 tsp. honey

Combine ingredients in a small bowl and pour over chunks of fresh pineapple, or orange slices and seedless grapes. This is also delicious on fresh strawberries or peaches.

Nutritional information per tbs. 20 calories, 0 grams fat, 0 grams saturated fat, 0 grams polyunsaturated fat, 0 grams monounsaturated fat, 0 grams protein, 5 grams carbohydrate, 0 mg cholesterol, 5 mg sodium

Elegant Strawberries

Long stem strawberries dipped in a little light sour cream and then in brown sugar make an easy and satisfying dessert to eat with your fingers. Chill the washed strawberries and put the brown sugar and light sour cream in separate little containers for dipping.

fresh washed strawberries with stems left on
1 tbs. light sour cream
1 tbs. brown sugar

No instructions needed. Dip the strawberries first in the sour cream and then in the brown sugar and pop into your mouth.

Nutritional information per serving 105 calories, 2 grams fat, 1 gram saturated fat, 0 grams polyunsaturated fat, 1 gram monounsaturated fat, 1 gram protein, 22 grams carbohydrate, 6 mg cholesterol, 14 mg sodium

---

Stuffed Dates

Use the flavorful Medjool or other large dried dates. They are easy to pit and really satisfy your sweet tooth.

4 dried dates
1 tbs. light cream cheese
¼ tsp. orange rind, grated
1 tbs. pecans, chopped

With a small knife cut from one end on one side to the center of the date and remove pit. Combine cream cheese with orange rind and pecans and stuff dates with mixture. Gently press date sides back together. Wrap in plastic or place in small carrying container.

Nutritional information per date   50 calories, 3 grams fat, 1 gram saturated fat, 0 grams polyunsaturated fat, 1 gram monounsaturated fat, 1 gram protein, 7 grams carbohydrate, 4 mg cholesterol, 11 mg sodium

Chocolate Biscotti

These are a nontraditional takeoff on the classic Italian cookie.

½ cup unsalted butter, melted
1 cup sugar
1 tsp. vanilla
1 tsp. chocolate extract
3 tbs. dark rum **or** Frangelico liqueur

3 eggs
2½ cups all purpose flour
3 tbs. cocoa
1½ tsp. baking powder
1 cup whole hazelnuts, toasted

Preheat oven to 350°. Mix butter, sugar, vanilla, chocolate extract and dark rum in a bowl. Whisk eggs in a small bowl until frothy and stir into butter-sugar mixture. Sift flour, cocoa and baking powder together, add to mixture and stir well to combine. Add hazelnuts. Form into two loaves about 3" wide and ¾" high on a well greased cookie sheet. Bake for 20-25 minutes until cake-like. The tops of loaves may crack. Remove from oven and allow to cool for 5-10 minutes. Cut loaves into ½" slices and place on cookie sheet. Return to oven for 10 minutes to crisp. Turn over and crisp the other side for an additional 10 minutes. Remove from oven and allow to cool. Store in an airtight container.

Note: To toast hazelnuts, put them in a jellyroll pan in a preheated 350° oven. Shake pan frequently. When nuts start to brown and begin to smell toasty, remove from oven and turn into a rough bath towel. Rub the nuts in the towel to loosen the brown skin. Remove as many skins as possible. Cool before adding to cookie dough.

Nutritional information per cookie 80 calories, 4 grams fat, 1 gram saturated fat, 0 grams polyunsaturated fat, 2 grams monounsaturated fat, 2 grams protein, 10 grams carbohydrate, 18 mg cholesterol, 30 mg sodium

Carrot Apple Cake

Grated carrots and apples help keep this dessert fresh tasting for several days.

1½ cups all purpose flour
1 tsp. baking powder
½ tsp. baking soda
½ tsp. ground ginger
1 tsp. cinnamon
½ tsp. nutmeg
½ tsp. salt
2 eggs
¾ cup sugar

½ cup vegetable oil
1 tsp. vanilla
⅓ cup milk
1 cup carrots, finely shredded
  (about 1 large)
1 cup apple, peeled, finely grated
  (about 1 small)
½ cup pecans, chopped

Preheat oven to 350°. Oil and lightly flour an 8" x 8" x 2" baking pan. Set aside. Sift together flour, baking powder, baking soda, ginger, cinnamon, nutmeg and salt. Place eggs in a mixer bowl; beat until light colored. Add sugar and oil to eggs; beat well. Stir in vanilla, milk and flour mixture. Add grated carrots, apple and pecans. Pour into prepared baking pan. Bake at 350° about

35-40 minutes, until toothpick or cake tester comes out clean. Cool on a rack. Dust with powdered sugar if desired. Cut into squares to serve.

Nutritional information per square 185 calories, 10 grams fat, 2 grams saturated fat, 4 grams polyunsaturated fat, 4 grams monounsaturated fat, 3 grams protein, 3 grams carbohydrate, 26 mg cholesterol, 60+ mg sodium

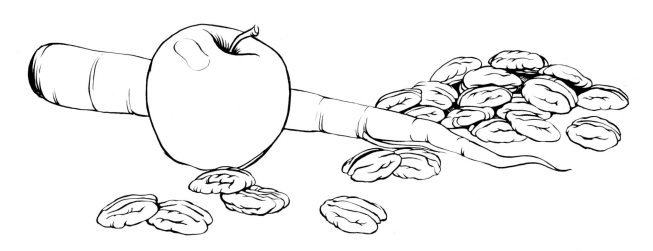

Lunch Box Brownies

These chocolate brownies are just the thing to tuck into the corner of the lunch box for a sweet treat.

2 (1 oz. each) squares unsweetened chocolate
¾ cup all purpose flour
½ tsp. baking powder
¼ tsp. salt
½ cup butter

¾ cup brown sugar
2 eggs
1 tsp. vanilla
½ cup walnuts, chopped
½ cup raisins

Preheat oven to 350°. Oil and lightly flour an 8" x 8" x 2" baking pan. Set aside. Melt chocolate squares over hot water or in a microwave. Sift flour, baking powder and salt together. Place butter in a mixer bowl; beat with sugar until well combined. Beat in chocolate, eggs and vanilla. Add flour mixture and combine. Stir in chopped nuts and raisins. Place in prepared baking pan. Bake at 350° for 25 minutes, or until toothpick or cake tester comes out clean. Place on a rack to cool. Cut into 16 squares when cool.

Nutritional information per brownie 175 calories, 11 grams fat, 5 grams saturated fat, 2 grams polyunsaturated fat, 3 grams monounsaturated fat, 3 grams protein, 20 grams carbohydrate, 42 mg cholesterol, 70 mg sodium

Banana Orange Cupcakes

Use very ripe bananas and bake in foil bake cups on a cookie sheet for a delicious out of hand dessert.

2 cups flour
1 tsp. baking soda
salt
2 eggs
⅓ cup peanut oil
⅔ cup brown sugar

1 tsp. vanilla
1 cup banana pulp, about 2-3 bananas
⅓ cup orange juice
grated rind from 1 orange
½ cup pecans, chopped, **or** walnuts

Preheat oven to 375°. Sift together flour, baking soda and salt. Set aside. Place eggs in a mixer bowl and beat until light colored. Add oil, brown sugar and vanilla and mix well. Stir in banana pulp, orange juice and orange rind. Add flour mixture and combine. Stir in nuts. Spoon into 16 cupcake forms, filling each about ⅔ full. Bake at 375° about 20 minutes, or until toothpick or cake tester comes out clean. Cool on a rack.

Nutritional information per cupcake 240 calories, 8 grams fat, 1 grams saturated fat, 3 grams polyunsaturated fat, 3 grams monounsaturated fat, 4 grams protein, 34 grams carbohydrate, 35 mg cholesterol, 90+ mg sodium

Frozen Fruit Cups

Put together fresh, frozen or canned pieces of fruit in a small airtight container and keep in freezer. If using some fresh fruit pieces be sure to include lemon or orange juice to keep the color bright. These also keep the lunch box nice and cool.

1 small orange, peeled, sliced		1 cup strawberries, sliced
1 cup pineapple slices		1 cup raspberries
1 cup strawberries, sliced	**or**:	½ cup blueberries
1 tsp. lemon **or** orange juice		½ cup canned **or** frozen peach slices
grated lemon **or** orange rind		1 tsp. lemon juice

Combine in small airtight containers and freeze or refrigerate.

Nutritional information per serving 100 calories, 1 gram fat, 0 grams saturated fat, 0 grams polyunsaturated fat, 0 grams monounsaturated fat, 1 gram protein, 25 grams carbohydrate, 0 mg cholesterol, 5 mg sodium

---

Figs and Prosciutto

Figs or pears are both delicious wrapped with a thin slice of prosciutto or Westphalian ham.

1 ripe fig, cut in half
lime juice
freshly ground pepper
1 thin slice prosciutto

Sprinkle fig halves with lime juice and freshly ground pepper. Cut prosciutto slice lengthwise and wrap around each fig half.

Nutritional information per serving 30 calories, 1 gram fat, 0 grams saturated fat, 0 grams polyunsaturated fat, 0 grams monounsaturated fat, 2 grams protein, 5 grams carbohydrate, 1 mg cholesterol, 100 mg sodium

---

Be creative! Use 1½" chunks of fresh pear, papaya or melon and wrap with prosciutto.

Marinated Strawberries

For some difficult-to-explain reason, the black pepper brings out the sweetness of the strawberries.

1 cup strawberries, sliced
1 tbs. orange juice
⅛ tsp. coarsely ground black pepper

Combine strawberries and orange juice. Sprinkle with black pepper. Refrigerate until ready to eat.

Nutritional information per serving 52 calories, 1 gram fat, 0 grams saturated fat, 0 grams polyunsaturated fat, 0 grams monounsaturated fat, 1 gram protein, 12 grams carbohydrate, 0 mg cholesterol, 2 mg sodium

---

Index